Extraordinary Animals

Extraordinary Animals

MARCUS SCHNECK

THE APPLE PRESS

A QUINTET BOOK

Published by The Apple Press
6 Blundell Street
London, N7 9BH

Reprinted 1991

Copyright © 1990 Quintet Publishing Limited.
All rights reserved. No part of this publication may
be reproduced, stored in a retrieval system or
transmitted in any form or by any means,
electronic, mechanical, photocopying, recording
or otherwise, without the permission of the
copyright holder.

ISBN 1-85076-235-X

Creative Director: Peter Bridgewater
Art Director: Ian Hunt
Designer: Stuart Walden, Sally McKay
Project Editor: David Game
Editor: Eleanor Van Zandt
Artwork by Danny McBride

Typeset in Great Britain by
Central Southern Typesetters, Eastbourne
Manufactured in Hong Kong by
Regent Publishing Services Limited
Printed in Hong Kong by
Leefung-Asco Printers Limited

Contents

Introduction 6
Giants and Miniatures 16
Bizarre Bodies 28
Defensive Postures 40
Special Abilities 58
The Next Generation 70
All the Colours of the Rainbow 78
The Builders 88
A Varied Menu 102
The Numbers Game 108
The Movers 110
At the Edge 116
Appendix (Endangered Species) 120
Further Reading 124
Index 125
Picture Credits 127

Introduction

Forget, for a moment, this man-made world of concrete, steel and glass where most of us live out the majority of our days. Clear your mind's eye of all the artificial constructions and constraints that humans have placed upon the earth. See only the place that this was before man 'civilized' it.

This is the natural world, in which every nook and cranny becomes a niche for some animal to fill and each niche is connected to every other niche in some way. One animal dies, another one eats. A forest grows older, the life within it adapts and changes.

In this sense every single place on earth is the same: the impenetrable rainforests of South America's Amazon River Basin, Central Park in New York City, the Alpine mountains of France, the central Channel Country of Australia, the boggy tundra of northern Canada, a back garden in suburban London, the Tunguska of Russia. They all must function according to this one natural principle. Except where man's interference is too severe, Nature will not permit a niche to go unused.

Every continent, every region, every locale holds its own set of niches – its ecosystem – which different animals and plants have come to exploit. And, in turn, they are exploited as part of that ecosystem, connected to every other creature's niche in some way or another. The exact occupants of the niche vary from one location to the next, but the niche itself remains across the spectrum.

Large herbivores (plant-eaters), for example, have evolved into an astonishing array of form and function across the globe to fill similar, if somewhat differing, niches. The white-tailed deer, with an ever-expanding range, is the representative for much of the United States and southeastern Canada, even in highly developed regions. Mule deer, moose and elk take over in the West, with the moose and elk extending north and east into Canada. Pronghorn antelope fill this position in some of the western open country. The mighty bison, which is greatly reduced in numbers today, at one time took advantage of grazing opportunities across the entire continent.

To the north, the barren ground-dwelling caribou survives by eating plants near the northernmost edge of the treeline and the open ground regions near the Artic Circle. To the south, the llama and alpaca range up into the 3,700- to 4,900-metre (12,0000- to 16,000-foot) elevations of the Andes Mountains.

RIGHT Large plant eaters have evolved on every continent, although in an incredible diversity of form. The white-tailed deer of most of North America is one of the few of these animals that are gaining significantly in the presence of man . . .

The muskox makes its way on just about any vegetation it comes across in Greenland. Red deer, although drastically reduced in numbers, roam forests in most of Europe. Reindeer take over the niche in some of the Scandinavian countries.

Giraffe, elephant, zebra, wildebeeste and gazelle rely on the vegetation of the African plains, sometimes at different levels and often in competition. The few remaining wild camels eke out their existence in arid regions to the north and in Asia, where other animals of similar size cannot find enough vegetation to exist.

Off the African coast, on the island of Madagascar, long-term isolation has thwarted the development of the larger herbivores, and a diversity of species of lemurs (arboreal primates) have branched out into these particular niches.

ABOVE . . . *Elk fill a similar niche in many areas . . .*

Similarly, Australia's isolation has prevented the introduction of many families of animal found elsewhere in the world. In their absence, many niches of its ecosystem have been taken up by species of marsupial. Some of the more than 50 species of kangaroo have evolved into the continent's largest herbivores.

Many other species that we have not named here occupy these very same niches, sometimes in competition with those we have described and sometimes non-competitively in other areas. Many more exist in other niches that those we've described could never occupy.

The purpose of this book is not to provide a detailed discussion of a single, identical niche in every possible ecosystem. Rather, it is an exploration of the amazing diversity of life that has developed over our planet to take advantage of all the richness it has to offer.

Some forms of life are more noticeable, more extraordinary, if you will. But every one of them, including ourselves, is moving ahead with a purpose which at its most basic can be summarized as finding and using those advantages that allow life to continue. Each has its own diversity, which may distinguish it only slightly, or considerably, from other forms. The earth supports an astonishing variety of extraordinary animals.

The spectrum of size alone ranges from the massive blue whale, which can grow to a length of 30 metres (100 feet), to microscopic spores – the whale being 10 million times the size of the protozoan spores.

Similar diversity can be found in every form and every function of the animal kingdom. Evolution and adaptation have brought about this diversity. They are the complex of processes that gave rise to the very first living things, organisms similar to modern-day bacteria which date to about 3.4 billion (i.e. 3,400,000,000) years ago. Along with giving the earth its amazing diversity of life, they have caused many other species to become extinct. And they continue today to diversify and modify all life.

The British naturalist Charles Darwin first gave voice to what the encyclopedias refer to as 'modern evolutionary theory' in his book *On the Origin of Species by Means of Natural Selection* published in 1859.

As an unpaid naturalist – his family was independently wealthy – aboard the *HMS Beagle* between 1831 and 1836, Darwin travelled the world as part of a scientific expedition. On the Galapagos Islands, off the western coast of equatorial South America, he observed the unique forms of life that had developed on the various islands, apparently from a few common beginnings.

He studied the amazing variations that had developed among the finches, tortoises and mockingbirds to allow them to fill the many niches of the ecosystems on the different islands. His term for what had happened there, and across the rest of the world, was 'natural selection'.

Darwin noted that offspring inherited a similarity to their parents, but not an identical similarity. Further-

LEFT . . . as does pronghorn antelope of the open grasslands . . .

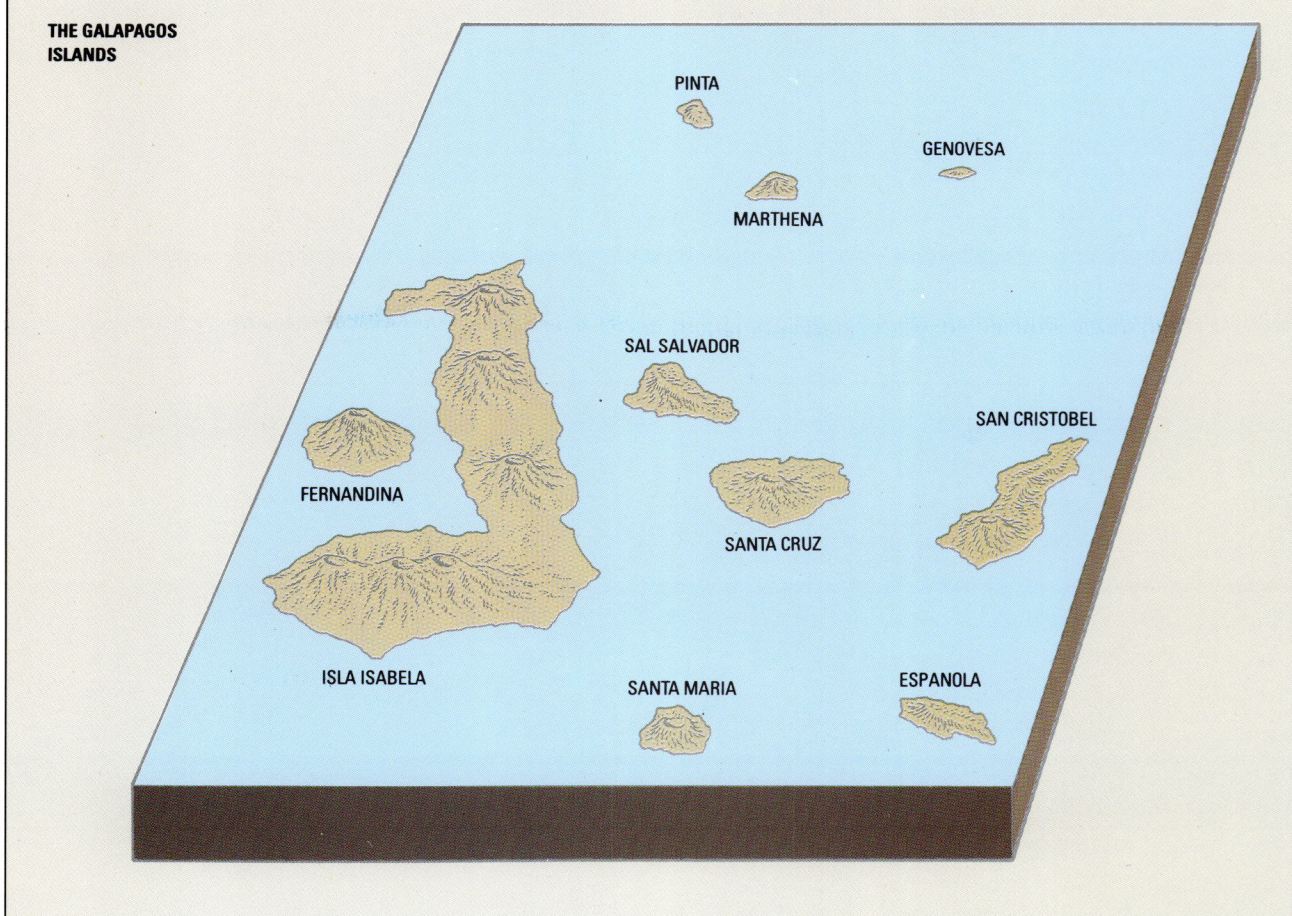

ABOVE . . . several different herbivores, including the giraffe, on the African plains . . .

LEFT Charles Darwin's theory of evolution was the product of his scientific study of the disparate development of species on the various Galapagos Islands, situated off the western coast of equatorial South America. He noted that amazing variations had developed among finches, tortoises and mockingbirds to allow them to adapt to the varied ecosystems on the different islands.

more, not all of the differences could be explained solely by environmental factors. Some of the variations gave individual offspring advantages that adapted the animals better to their environments or enabled them to create more offspring. Since more offspring are produced than can survive to produce additional offspring, there is a selection process that favours those that are more fit for their environment.

Over generations this natural selection can give rise to an advantageous adaptation across a population. It can, and has, also led down the blind alley to extinction of a population.

In this manner, the genetic code of reproduction is exact for enough of the time to bring a stability to a species, but inexact often enough to produce change, however small. According to Darwin, '... favourable variations would tend to be preserved, and unfavourable ones to be destroyed .... More individuals are born than can possibly survive. A grain in the balance can determine which individuals shall live and which shall die.'

When, however, an organism is already well adapted to its environment and circumstances, chances are good that these mutations will lead to individuals that are less well adapted and thus fall by the wayside – thus preventing a population 'explosion'. Crocodiles and cockroaches, both much the same as they appear to have been some 300 million years ago, are examples of fully adapted species.

Environmental changes are another part of this puzzle, to which animals must either adapt, use the adaptations that they have or become extinct. Scientists have delineated at least five mass extinctions in the history of life on earth, the most famous of which is the passing of the dinosaurs about 65 million years ago.

Needless to say, Darwin's theory created a uproar when it was offered to a society that held that each species was created exactly in its present form and neither could nor would ever change. The scientific community, of course, included many opponents to the new way of thinking, but the most vehement opposition came from the religious community. Statements such as 'There is no fundamental difference between man and the higher animals in their mental faculties,' obviously did not endear Darwin to orthodox believers. Nor did: 'We must, however, acknowledge, as it seems to me, that man with all his noble qualities ... still bears in his bodily frame the indelible stamp of his lowly origin.'

ABOVE *The crocodile has changed very little over the past 300 million years indicating that it is one of the few species fully adapted to its environment.*

RIGHT *... and the kangaroo of Australia.*

LEFT On the Galapagos Islands, Charles Darwin encountered such puzzling creatures as blue-footed boobie.

RIGHT In evolutionary theory, man and chimpanzee are quite closely related, a statement that continues to draw heated debate even today.

The debate continues today. Admittedly, Darwin's theory, the subsequent sub-theories and the alternative theories that have been proposed do not explain all the nuances of the entire diversity of life today and how it came to this point. However, they offer the most plausible explanation; and in science, plausibility is the crucial factor.

Chance must play some part in the process. Some adaptations that developed to cope with one environental challenge are probably used for something quite different today. For example, fish living millennia ago in water that from time to time became quite low in oxygen probably developed the first lungs to deal with that situation. Later, it turned out, they were adapted to make the move onto land, to exploit a new possibility, a new advantage.

Co-adaptation also accounts for some of the diversity, advancing two or more species in concert with one another. Flower-bearing plants and the animals that carry the plants' pollen at some point moved ahead together through their independent, yet connected, developments. Predator and prey display similarly linked advancement. In short, no animal exists in isolation from others. It simply cannot.

Isolated ecosystems, such as Australia and the island of Madagascar, demonstrate another of the processes of diversity. The scientific term for this process is 'adaptive radiation'. It describes the fact that the available species of animal, and other life, will evolve and branch out to fill the available niches within the ecosystem.

In their relative isolation, in the absence of many other forms of life, the marsupials of Australia (of which kangaroos are just one example) and the lemurs of Madagascar have evolved to perform all the roles of living – predator and prey, arboreal and terrestrial, and so on.

This is not to say that all present animal life arose from a single series of organisms advancing gradually

EXTRAORDINARY ANIMALS

Through co-adaptation, different species evolve in concert with one another, such as flower-bearing plants and the honeybees that garner their nourishment from the plants while spreading their pollen.

FAR RIGHT Man, himself, has become a pressure of sorts in the continuing evolution on life on earth. He generally has not been a positive factor, driving species such as the Florida panther to the brink of extinction.

from the lower forms to the higher forms, like a single branch of a tree. Instead, evolution is a tree with many branches, each going through its own adaptive radiation and diversification. Evolution is progressing across the animal kingdom along different routes.

Thus we arrive at the current world's supply of several million species, possibly more still to be discovered than we have already catalogued. To manage the study of such diversity, science has classified all life into five major groups, or kingdoms. They are:

— Kingdom Monera. One-celled organisms without membranes around their genetic material.
— Kingdom Protoctista. One-celled organisms that have membranes around their genetic material.
— Kingdom Fungi. One-celled or multi-celled organisms with cells that have membranes around their genetic material (eucaryotic cells), but do not produce their own food.
— Kingdom Plantae. Multi-celled organisms with eucaryotic cells that produce their food through photosynthesis – in other words, plants.
— Finally, the kingdom with which this book is concerned: Kingdom Animalia. These are multi-celled organisms with eucaryotic cells which ingest their food.

Within each kingdom, life is further divided into smaller and smaller groupings, based on comparisons of features such as genetics, anatomy, behaviour, function, fossil history and ecology. The next classification down from kingdom is phylum. The phylum *Mollusca*, for example, includes such animals as snails, clams and octopi. *Arthropoda* includes creatures such as spiders, insects and crabs. *Chordata* includes fish, amphibians, reptiles, birds and mammals, including man.

Such elaborate classification is made necessary by the sheer diversity of life on earth. The current supply is placed at several million species, with possibly more of them still undiscovered than known.

In recent history (relative to the earth's lifespan) a new pressure has been brought to bear on the diversity of life – a pressure that works primarily against diversity. That force is man. In the short time that the human race has been civilized, we have managed, according to some estimates, to wipe as many species from the face of the earth as disappeared during the dinosaurs' extinction.

Many more species are endangered – primarily by man's activities – beyond the point of no return. Some observers predict that the earth will lose about 20 per cent of its species in the next 20 years. Some of the animals discussed in the rest of this book, some of the most extraordinary creatures in existence, won't be with us as we begin the 21st century.

The following pages, however, are intended mainly as a celebration of the diversity of animal life through some of the most remarkable examples, with perhaps some thought towards allowing them to continue.

EXTRAORDINARY ANIMALS

Giants and Miniatures

BELOW & BELOW RIGHT Most animals give the elephant wide birth because of its size and strength. The mighty creature, however, is prey to one relentless predator – man. The elephant's ivory tusks have lured hunters over the ages and this precious material can still command $100 (£64) per pound. Despite vigorous conservation programmes implemented over the past ten years, poaching is still widespread and during this period alone the total worldwide elephant population has fallen dramatically from 1.3 million to just 400,000. Unless this decimation of the population is reversed the elephant may no longer exist in the wild by the year 2000.

Size is one of the most instantly recognized and most amazing diversities in the animal kingdom. From the 30-metre (100-foot) blue whale to the 3/25,000 of an inch protozoan spore (the smallest thing recognized as an animal), there is a 10 million-fold drop in size. An astonishing number of niches can be filled by the creatures that occupy such a large range.

The largest animal ever to exist is the blue whale, which can be as long as 30 metres (100 feet) and weigh as much as 125 tons. Even the longest dinosaur – the diplodocus, which became extinct millions of years ago – was a comparatively short 24 metres (80 feet) in length.

A newborn calf of the blue whale can be more than 7.6 metres (25 feet) in length and weigh as much as 3 tons. That same calf can weigh as much as 26 tons 12 months later, following a year of the most rapid growth in the entire animal and plant kingdoms.

Despite its massive bulk, the blue whale's diet consists of shrimp-sized crustaceans known as krill, a ton of which are needed to fill its great stomach. The whale strains the tiny creatures from the seawater through sheets of whalebone (baleen) in its mouth.

The blue whale's terrestrial counterpart in the size hierarchy is the elephant, which doesn't seem all that large when compared to the bulk of the whale. Nevertheless, the elephant is today's giant among all land-based animals.

RIGHT The African elephant is the largest terrestrial animal alive today. A bull might weigh six tons.

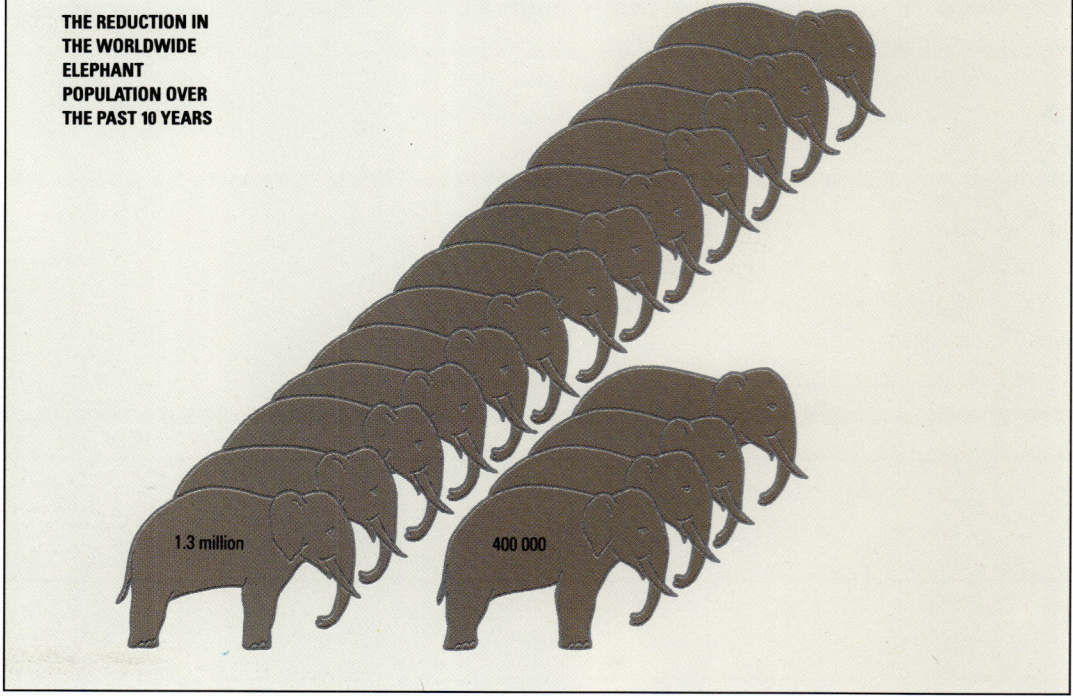

THE REDUCTION IN THE WORLDWIDE ELEPHANT POPULATION OVER THE PAST 10 YEARS

1.3 million   400 000

16

An average bull African elephant stands nearly 3.2 metres (10½ feet) at the shoulder and weighs about 6 tons. The smaller Asian elephant is about 2.7 metres (9 feet) at the shoulder and 5 tons.

Far above the average, however, is the largest recorded African bull elephant. Shot in late 1955 in Angola, this animal stood 3.8 metres (12½ feet) at the shoulder and weighed more than 10 tons. This Fenykoevi elephant (so-named for the successful hunter) is on display just inside the entrance to the U.S. National Museum of Natural History, in Washington, D.C.

The largest bull elephant kept in captivity was Jumbo, whose owner – Phineas T. Barnum – claimed that it was 3.7 metres (12 feet) tall at the shoulder. The showman never allowed measurements to be taken, but evidence seems to suggest a shoulder height of closer to 3.4 metres (11 feet). Jumbo, who was originally captured south of Lake Chad, in Africa, died on 15 September 1885, after being struck by a train in Ontario, Canada.

The sheer mass of a creature such as the blue whale and the elephant is their greatest defence against all natural enemies. Only rarely is a healthy adult of either species brought down by any natural predator, although sick, injured and young specimens ones may be.

Nevertheless, man – the most efficient predator ever – has pushed both whales and elephants precipitously close to oblivion. The impressive bulk of the animal is as nothing before the formidable array of weaponry that man has developed to penetrate and destroy that bulk.

In the past 10 years, despite rigorous protection efforts, poachers have reduced the world's population of elephants from more than 1.3 million to less than 400,000. There is even some speculation that the elephant will not exist in the wild in the next century.

Poaching incentives are strong. On the $1.5 billion (£780 million) worldwide trade circuit for animals and animal parts, elephant tusk ivory fetches a minimum of $100 (£64) per pound.

Not poaching, but legal whaling operations have had a similar impact on all whale species, including the massive blue whale. The total world population of blue whales is estimated at only a few thousand – barely a memory of the 200,000 that probably roamed the earth's oceans before the advent of commercial whaling. They are divided among three races: northern, in the North Atlantic and North Pacific oceans; southern, throughout the southern hemisphere; and pygmy, in the southern Indian Ocean and Antarctic waters, this last form was discovered only in 1961.

The largest fish in the oceans, the whale shark, has not come under the same degree of intense exploitation as the whales. This gentle giant lives on tiny plankton

ABOVE *The giant squid, a cousin of this small squid that washed up on a beach in Maine, has given rise to much nautical folklore. Attacks on man are extremely rare, and are even more rarely authenticated, by the giant which can grow to nearly 17 metres (55 feet) in length from head to tentacle.*

BELOW *In contrast to the plight of the elephant, the decimation of the blue whale population has been caused by legal commercial hunting operations.*

BELOW *The giraffe, with a potential height of six metres (19 feet), is the tallest of all animals.*

LEFT *With its great height advantage, the giraffe can browse at the tops of trees on the African plains, far above the reach of any competitors.*

RIGHT However, for a drink at a water hole, the giraffe must put itself at a great disadvantage, awkwardly spreading its long legs.

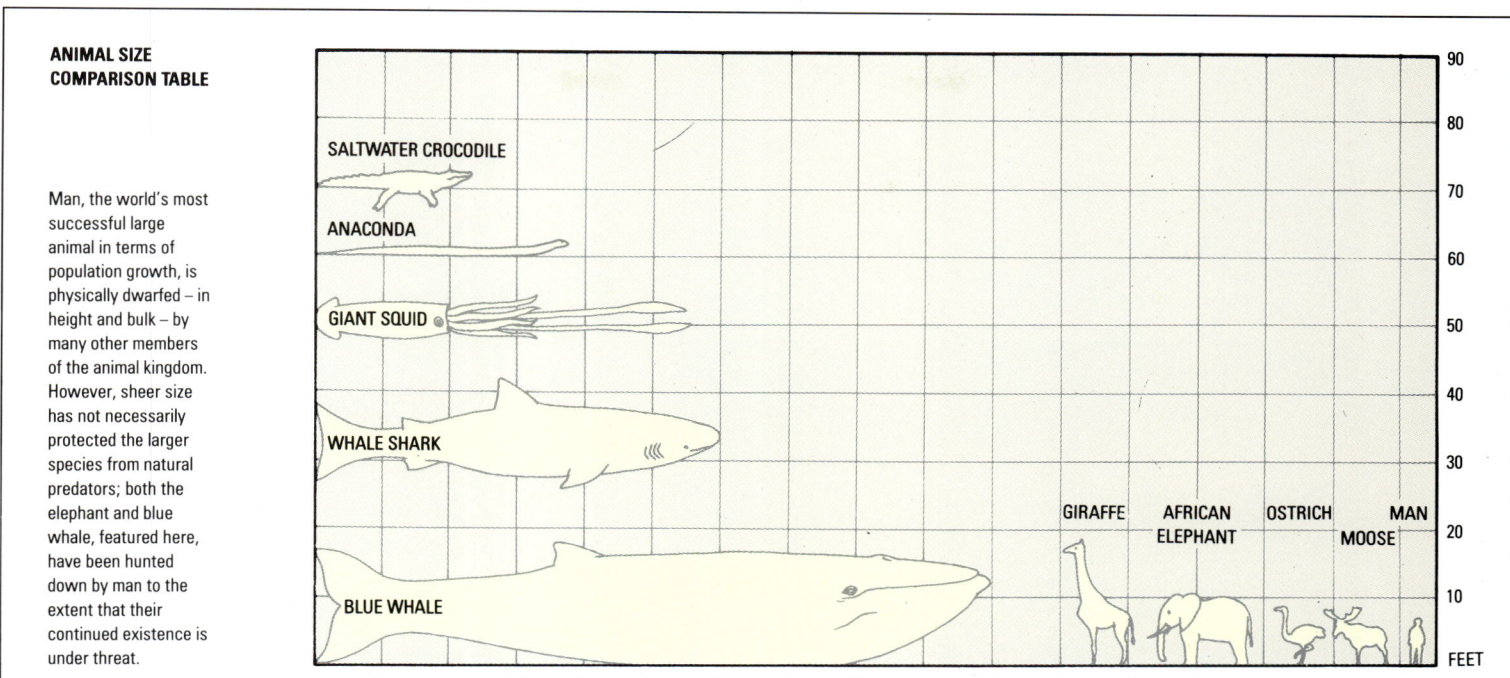

ANIMAL SIZE COMPARISON TABLE

Man, the world's most successful large animal in terms of population growth, is physically dwarfed – in height and bulk – by many other members of the animal kingdom. However, sheer size has not necessarily protected the larger species from natural predators; both the elephant and blue whale, featured here, have been hunted down by man to the extent that their continued existence is under threat.

which it filters from the water through the mesh of its gill rakes. An enormous amount is needed to sustain one of these 18-metre (60-foot) giants, which can weigh as much as 50 tons.

The oceans – which can seem the most foreign and formidable environment to land-loving man – and its strange, gigantic creatures have given rise to much folk-lore about giant creatures.

Apart from the sharks, no sea creature has inspired more awe and fear in man than the giant squid. Although a few attacks on humans have been documented, many early sailors' tales about the horn-beaked, tentacled animal sinking large ships were exaggerations at best. But the size of these giants gives us a hint of the origins of the tales. The largest giant squid ever recorded had a body 6 metres (20 feet) in length and tentacles that extended 10.7 metres (35 feet).

Likewise, tales of a man-eating giant clam have never been documented. However, the largest of these – a 264 kilogram (580-pound) specimen with a shell that measured 115 by 74 centimetres (45 by 29 inches) – could certainly hold a hapless diver or swimmer as long as it had a mind to.

The largest pearl ever collected from one of these clams is the Pearl of Laotze, a brain-shaped specimen which weighs slightly more than 6.4 kilograms (14 pounds) and has a diameter of 14 centimetres (5½ inches). It was collected in the Philippines in 1934.

BELOW The moose of northern and western North America is the largest deer on earth. Specimens of more than 1100 kg (2,500 pounds) have been taken.

21

ABOVE *Standing as tall as three metres (nine feet), the ostrich is the largest bird alive today. The 155 kg (345-pound) giant cannot fly.*

FAR RIGHT *A close relative to man, the lowland gorilla of Africa can weigh as much as 160 kg (360 pounds). The animal is, deceptively, extremely non-violent.*

For the maximum height in the animal world, we must return to land. With a potential height of 5.8 metres (19 feet), a full-grown male giraffe could look down on the whale, if such an impossible encounter were to take place.

The giraffe puts this height to use on the dry plains of south and central Africa, where it can browse on vegetation far beyond the reach of its competitors. A tongue that can extend as much as 45 centimetres (1½ feet) affords even more reach.

However the giraffe's size is not without a price. To stoop for a drink of water, the giant must spread its legs wide into a straddled position. In this position, the giraffe is at its most vulnerable to attack from predators.

The North American bull moose is the largest deer in the world. An average-sized, adult bull moose can stand more than 2 metres (6 feet) at the withers and weigh as much as 545 kilograms (1,200 pounds). Hunters have killed specimens of more than 2.1 metres (7 feet) and 1,140 kilograms (2,500 pounds).

The pudu of South American is the moose's 'smallest' counterpart. It is 38 centimetres (15 inches) at the withers and weighs 9 kilograms (20 pounds). Southeast Asia's mouse deer, 25 centimetres (10 inches) at the withers and seven pounds, is smaller, but it has only three compartments to its stomach, rather than four and thus is not a true deer.

Looming over any of the deer is the ostrich, the largest of all birds, with a height of as much as 2.7 metres (9 feet). This flightless giant of Africa and southwest Asia can weigh as much as 157 kilograms (345 pounds).

Even this size, however, seems moderate in comparison to the now-extinct moa of New Zealand, a bird that probably stood 4 metres (13 feet) tall. The elephant bird of Madagascar, also extinct, was about the size of the largest ostrich today.

The ostrich lays an egg that measures as much as 20 centimetres (8 inches) from end to end, weighs nearly 1.8 kilograms (4 pounds) and could hold several of the tiny buzz-bombs at the other end of the bird-size spectrum, the bee hummingbird.

Native to Cuba and the Isle of Pines, the average bee hummingbird is only 5.5 centimetres (2¼ inches) from tip of beak to tip of tail. The tiny bird, the world's smallest, weighs about 21 grams (¾ ounce). Into a nest about the size of a thimble, it lays eggs that are about 1 centimetre (less than ½ inch) from end to end and weigh less than 5.7 grams (⅕ ounce).

The smallest flightless bird is only slightly larger. The flightless rail, of Inaccessible Island, in the South Atlantic, is about the size of a freshly hatched chicken. It is a swift runner and spends much of its time in burrows.

Nearly as small as the flightless rail is the musk shrew, the tiniest member of the most diminutive family of mammals. With a body measuring less than 5 centimetres (2 inches) long and a tail of about 2.5 centimetres

LEFT North America's brown bear is the largest terrestrial carnivore. These three bears, which are known as grizzly bears, have gathered at the McNeil River in Alaska for the spawning "run" of the salmon.

BELOW Detail of the tiger's markings.

(1 inch), the animal weighs less than an American dime, and considerably less than a British 1p. It can pass through tunnels made by earthworms.

The 150 species of shrew make up the smallest group of mammals, although their largest representative – the hero shrew of tropical Africa – can be as much as 23 centimetres (9 inches) long. Because of the interlocked vertebrae in its spine, the large shrew is also quite strong. It can support an average-sized man on its back.

Each family of animals seems to produce its giants – relative, at least to the other members of the family. On man's branch of the evolutionary tree, the primates, the honours must go to the eastern lowland gorilla of Zaire and Uganda. An adult bull can weigh 164 kilograms (360 pounds), have a chest girth of 150 centimetres (60 inches) and stand (fully erect) 1.7 metres (5 feet 9 inches) tall.

Unconfirmed claims of 2.14-metre (7-foot), 320-kilogram (700-pound) bull gorillas notwithstanding, the largest reliably recorded weight is 219 kilograms (482 pounds), and the tallest accurate measurement is 1.85 metres (6 feet 2 inches.).

The largest meat-eating mammal on land is the brown bear of North America. These bears average about 450 kilograms (1,000 pounds), although a 753-kilogram (1,656-pound) specimen was shot on Kodiak Island, in the Gulf of Alaska, in 1894, and one weighing 760 kilograms (1,670-pounds) died in 1955 in the

BELOW The Siberian tiger, the largest member of the cat family, can grow to more than three metres (ten feet) in length and 270 kg (600 pounds) in weight.

FAR RIGHT The Atlas silk moth of Asia is the largest moth, with a wingspan of more than 25cm (10 inches).

ABOVE The largest rodent on earth is the capybara of South America. Individuals, such as this one in a zoo, can weigh as much as 80 kg (175 pounds).

Cheyenne Mountain Zoological Park in Colorado.

A larger polar bear – weighing 1,005 kilograms (2,210 pounds), – was killed by a hunter in northwest Alaska, and other polar bear weights have been estimated in excess of 820 kilograms (1,800 pounds). But the average white bear weighs about 410 kilograms (900 pounds).

The largest member of the cat family is the long-furred Siberian tiger. On average, the male stands 107 centimetres (42 inches) at the shoulder, is more than 3 metres (10 feet) long and weighs nearly 275 kilograms (600 pounds). The African lion, on the other hand, stands 97 centimetres (38 inches) at the shoulder, is about 2.75 metres (10 feet) long and weighs about 180 kilograms (400 pounds).

By contrast, the smallest meat-eating mammal, the least weasel of Siberia, is just 18 centimetres (7 inches) long and weighs 65 grams (2½ ounces) at most. For its size, however, this small weasel is extremely ferocious.

In the limited family of marsupials, the red kangaroo of Australia is the giant. The animal has been measured at 2.75 metres (9 feet) along the curve of its body and weighed in at about 90 kilograms (200 pounds).

A much more widespread and common family is made up of the rodents, the largest of which is the capybara of South America. Large males can measure 1.4 metres (4½ feet) in length and weigh as much as 80 kilograms (175 pounds). The North American beaver is the next largest rodent, of which some males have weighed 40 kilograms (90 pounds).

The giant among the reptiles is the saltwater crocodile of southern Asia and northern Australia. Although unconfirmed reports place this creature's length at more than 6.7 metres (22 feet), the average is closer to 4.5 metres (15 feet), with a weight of 500 kilograms (1,100 pounds). Older specimens may be half-again as big.

Unconfirmed evidence also seems to show that much larger individuals – as long as 10 metres (33 feet) – existed before the creature came under the heavy persecution of man in this century.

The smallest of the 23 species of crocs, the Congo dwarf crocodile is a pygmy compared to its saltwater cousin. It never exceeds 114 centimetres (3 feet 9 inches).

In terms of sheer length, rather than overall body size, the saltwater crocodile is dethroned by a fellow reptile, the anaconda. Although the title of largest species of snake has been much debated, this South American constrictor is the most likely candidate.

An engineering party in Colombia recorded a length of more than 11.3 metres (37 feet) for one individual that it killed. Although the carcass was not weighed, an estimate of 450 kilograms (1,000 pounds) seems fair.

Among the lizards, the largest living species is the Komodo dragon, which inhabits the Indonesian island of the same name. A type of monitor lizard, the dragon can be 3 metres (10 feet) long and weigh more than 135 kilograms (300 pounds). Included among its prey are small deer and pigs.

The Komodo dragon stands precariously on the brink of extinction. It has been heavily hunted by man, but scarcity of food brought about through man's development of its habitat is now the most immediate threat.

The giants of the world of insects and arachnids can't compete in sheer size alone, but compared on their own scale they are nonetheless impressive.

For example, the Goliath beetle of central Africa, the heaviest insect, weighs in at 99 grams (3½ ounces), about the same as a small apple.

Some of the tropical stick insects are the longest of the insect family; a maximum of 33 centimetres (13 inches) is achieved by some adult females, which are larger than the males. By contrast, the smallest insect, the hairy-winged dwarf beetle, seems almost non-existent with its total length of less than 2.5 millimetres (1/10 inch).

The largest spider is the bird-eating spider of South America, with a leg span of as much as 25 centimetres (10 inches) and a body length of up to 9 centimetres (3½ inches). The hundreds of species of spider range from this maximum down to a minimum of slightly more than 2.5 millimetres (1/10 of an inch), the Patu marplesi of the southwest Pacific.

An aerial web, spun by the tropical orb weaver spiders

qualifies as the largest web. Some have been measured at more than 1.5 metres (5 feet) in diameter, with supporting guide-lines as long as 6 metres (20 feet).

The largest fly is the robber fly of tropical South America, with a body length of more than 6.5 centimetres (2½ inches); the largest wasp, the spider-hunting wasp of Amazonia, 6.5 centimetres (2½ inches) plus a 1.2 centimetre (½ inch) stinger; the largest butterfly, the Queen Alexandra birdwing of New Guinea, with a wingspan of more than 28 centimetres (11 inches); the largest moth, the Hercules emperor moth of Australia and New Guinea, with a wingspan of more than 27 centimetres (10½ inches).

Finally, there are those few creatures that don't seem to be sure which size is best for them. The warm-ocean fish known collectively as puffers are a prime example. The largest of these fish is about 60 centimetres (2 feet) long, but most are less than half that size. When threatened, a puffer gulps in water, air or both (depending on the species of puffer) and inflates its body to discourage attack. When the danger passes, the fish belches out the air or water to deflate to its normal size.

Bizarre Bodies

The long stream of successful mutations and adaptations has given us an animal kingdom filled with an almost inconceivable array of distinctive limbs, body parts and organs.

Some animals have been endowed with such bizarre bodies as to appear the work, not of Nature, but of a committee. When the platypus, for example, was first described to the scientific community in the late 1700s, the general consensus was that this peculiar animal was some sort of hoax.

Decades later, after the scientists had accepted the creature as real, they still weren't certain exactly where to classify this creature, with the beak and webbed feet of a duck, the flat tail of a beaver, the tiny black eyes of a mole and sharp venom-filled spines on its hind legs. To cloud the issue further, it was discovered that the platypus lays eggs, like a bird.

Despite its odd collection of body parts, the platypus functions quite well in its watery environment in Aus-

BELOW The elephant's trunk, powerfully muscled but still able to perform delicate functions, is intricately involved in much of the animal's daily life. This captive Asiatic elephant is working with its trainer at the Elephant Training Camp near Chiang Mai in Thailand.

RIGHT With their fully rotating eyes, chameleons, like this Meller's chameleon, can look in two different directions at the same time.

ABOVE *Because of their pachyderm-like noses, the African mormyrids have been given the common name of elephant-nose.*

tralia and Tasmania. For example, the leathery, yet sensitive, duck-bill serves well in rooting through the mud and sand for the animal's food.

We can see similar utility of design throughout the animal kingdom. The elephant's nose – its trunk – is as well designed for its life as is the nose of the platypus.

The elephant's elongated, mobile nose can weigh as much as 23 kilograms (250 pounds) and extend as long as 2.1 metres (7 feet). It is equipped with an intricate set of powerful muscles which enable it to lift large logs. And yet the elephant can also use its trunk to pick up tiny twigs and gently caress other members of its family.

The trunk enters into most daily functions of the elephant's life. The sense of smell, through the nostrils located at the tip of the double-tubed instrument, is much more acute than our own. The loud trumpeting call is produced by expelling air through the trunk. Water is drawn into it from watering holes or rivers – as much as 7.5 litres (1.6 British gallons) at a time – and squirted into the elephant's mouth.

An appendage similar to that of the elephant has evolved in a group of African fishes, known collectively as the mormyrids or elephant-noses. Although the 'nose' of one of these fish is actually its strangely projecting mouth, the design is equally important, for the fish uses it to probe among the gravel for its food.

The mormyrids, some as large as 1.5 metres (5 feet) long but most about 15 centimetres (6 inches), have

RIGHT *The 22 points of the star-nosed mole's nose help the small creature to find its way and its food.*

developed a further device to aid them in their search for food. Muscles near the base of the tail generate weak charges of electricity, which the fish apparently use in locating prey, rather than as a weapon.

Some of the billfishes, notably the swordfish, have developed a much more proactive nose extension. When a swordfish feeds, it charges through a school of fish, swinging its bill – which can be as much as a third of the fish's maximum 4.6 metre (15-foot) length – from side to side. It then turns back and gulps down any injured fish.

The sawfish – actually a species of ray – sports an equally effective nasal weapon which is edged on each side with a row of 18 or so sharp spines. The saw is used to rummage through the sand of the ocean bottom for prey, to club prey and to impale prey when thrashed back and forth through a school of fish.

Another strange variation on the nose is the 22-point proboscis of the North American star-nosed mole. The points – actually tentacle-like, fleshy projections – are used to help the mole move about and find food.

As the mole forages for prey, such as its favourite earthworms, the projections move constantly. But while it eats, they are held motionless and out of the way.

Marine proboscis worms make similar use of their tubular appendages, which can be extended rapidly to clutch prey or to ward off predators. In the case of prey, such as smaller worms, the proboscis worm then wraps itself around its victim, ensnaring it in mucus that can poison. In some species of this group of ribbon worms the proboscis carries a small spike which pierces the victim to allow easier access of the lethal poison.

These worms – a few species of which can be as long as 27 metres (90 feet) – also use their proboscis to burrow in the ocean floor and to grasp stationary objects to pull themselves along.

ABOVE *The hugely overgrown incisors, commonly known as tusks, are at once a tool for daily life and the greatest threat to the elephant. Man's lust for the ivory may well kill off all wild elephants by the turn of the century.*

FAR RIGHT *When extended, the sticky tongue of the chameleon is longer than the reptile's body. This is a Meller's chameleon of east Africa.*

The proboscis monkey of Borneo similarly takes its name from the flabby, pouchlike nose found on males, which hangs over the mouth, although this appendage seems to have fewer uses than on similarly endowed species. In some older males the nose is as long as 18 centimetres (7 inches), whereas the nose of the female is short and stubby. The snout's principal use appears to be in resonating the mating and warning calls.

The 6.7 metre (22-foot) bull elephant seal also uses its sac-like snout as a resonator for the wide range of bellows and snorts which it makes to announce its dominance over territory and a herd of as many as 50 cows. In older bulls the snout can be as long as 60 centimetres (2 feet). It can stand almost vertical when inflated with air.

Although the nose can be a prominent feature, it is obviously far from the only specialized body part that has developed into extreme forms. Teeth, for example, have developed to astounding proportions in some species.

Here again, the elephant is a classic example, for the tusks that have made this great beast so pursued by poachers are actually vastly overgrown incisors. The largest pair of tusks on record measured more than 3.3 metres (11 feet) each. Although these tusks, taken from an elephant killed in Zaire, were the longest, their combined weight of 133 kilograms (293 pounds) place them far from the heaviest. That record is held by the 209-kilogram (461-pound) pair of the 'Kilimanjaro elephant.'

These extremes have all been recorded in African elephants. The Asian elephants, which themselves are smaller, produce smaller tusks. A pair measuring more than 2.7 metres (9 feet) are the largest ever found.

A species of whale, the narwhal, also develops a frontal appendage from a tooth. This whale is born with a few stumpy teeth, all of which it eventually loses except the upper left canine tooth in males, and occasionally females. This tooth (sometimes both canine teeth) develops into a spear measuring as much as 3.4 metres (11 feet) in length and about 18 centimetres (7 inches) in diameter at the base.

Whether the narwhal uses its unicorn-like spear to attack prey – as the swordfish and sawfish use their extended noses – is not known.

RIGHT Antlers, such as these collected from a herd of fallow deer, grow anew each year, while horns are grown over the lifetime of the animal.

ABOVE The water buffalo of India and southeast Asia grows the largest horns of any animal. The largest measured three metres (14 feet).

ABOVE The chameleon is distinguished by its amazing long tongue, which is usually longer than the creature's entire body. Used to garner food, the tongue uncoils from the mouth, whipping out to catch an unwary insect on its sticky tip.

The tusks of the walrus are also greatly elongated upper canine teeth, as long as 1 metre (3 feet) in older males. And, like the tusks of the elephant, this ivory has led to massive reductions in the worldwide population through hunting by man.

Walruses use their tusks to rake the ocean floor in search of shellfish, the animals' dietary mainstay; to fight for dominance, among males; to protect themselves and others of the herd; and to climb over ice.

For some animals, the tongue has developed into an equally formidable tool. The chameleon – actually about 50 different species ranging from the 2.5 centimetre (1 inch) long dwarf chameleon to the 60-centimetre (2-foot) Oustalet's chameleon – is the prime specimen. In most species the tongue is longer than the entire animal from tip of nose to tip of tail. When the reptile locates a prey insect, the tongue uncoils from the mouth at lightning speed, shooting out the sticky bulging tip to snag the morsel.

The anteaters, including the scale-covered pangolins, make use of similarly sticky and long (though shorter

EXTRAORDINARY ANIMALS

RIGHT The moose sports the greatest antlers. This large bull has rubbed nearly all the velvet from his new set.

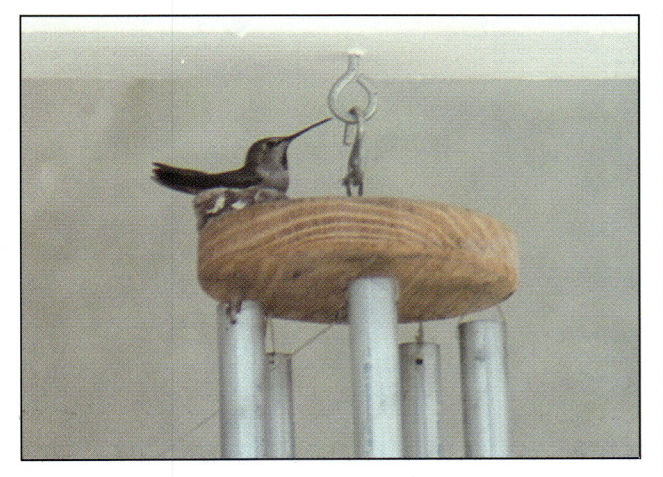

ABOVE *Yaks grow the thickest and longest hair of any animal. These domesticated yaks are part of a caravan travelling along a narrow mountain trail in Nepal.*

than those of the chameleons) tongues to lap up ants and termites after ripping into the insects' nests with heavily clawed front feet.

Another strange development around the mouth occurs in the skimmer bird, of which there are three species: black, along the Atlantic coast of the Americas; Indian, along the coasts of India and southern Asia; and African, along the coasts and inland shores of Africa.

The lower bill of a skimmer bird is nearly half as long again as the upper bill, a configuration unique among all birds. In addition, the lower bill is quite flat.

The bird flies quite close to the surface of the water, with the lower bill skimming that surface. When it strikes something, preferably a food item such as a small fish or shrimp, the upper bill closes on it. The bird's neck

ABOVE LEFT *Despite their tiny size, hummingbirds have relatively more feathers than all other birds.*

ABOVE *Dragonflies have compound eyes made up of many facets. Some have as many as 30,000 facets per eye.*

RIGHT *Because of their eye placement, rabbits, such as this young cottontail of eastern North America, can see almost everything on all sides without moving their heads.*

BELOW *The eyes of the starfish are located at the end of each of its five "points".*

muscles are unusually enlarged to provide a cushion for the shock involved in this form of fishing.

Horns and antlers are the extraordinary distinguishing characteristic for other species. Although these protuberances are popularly supposed to be the same, they are in fact quite different.

Horns are made of the same protein as fingernails, keratin. They are permanent and sprout on both sexes. Cattle, goats, antelope and bison are among the species with horns.

Antlers, on the other hand, are living bone. They are grown and shed on an annual cycle. The male is much more likely to grow them, although unusually high levels of testosterone can and do produce antlers on some females. Deer, elk and moose are the antlered species.

The largest horns of any animal belong to the Indian buffalo. A record spread of 4.3 metres (14 feet) from tip to tip was set by a bull killed by a hunter in 1955. Other massive, although lesser, spreads have been recorded in the Texas longhorn, 3.7 metres (12 feet), and the Ankole cattle of Africa, 3 metres (10 feet). The greatest antler span belongs to the largest member of the deer family, the moose. The average 'rack' measures 1.2 to 1.5 metres (4 to 5 feet) in width, but a spread of 2.3 metres (7½ feet) has been documented.

The smallest antlered animal is the pudu of northern South America. It stands about 33 centimetres (13 inches) at the shoulder and weighs about 7.7 kilograms (17 pounds).

Another of the smaller deer species, the 58 centimetre (23-inch)-tall musk deer of Asia, produces no antlers in either sex. In their place, the male grows long tusks which extend down from the mouth.

While the shaggy yak of the higher Asian mountains cannot compete at either extreme in the horn/antler category, this massive beast distinguishes itself by growing the thickest and longest coat of hair of any animal. The heavy protection serves the animal well in its cold, mountainous home – as high as 7,600 metres (25,000 feet) above sea level – but renders it unable to survive for long under lower, warmer conditions.

The avian world's equivalent of the yak in terms of natural covering might be the whistling swan. Recorded counts have found more than 25,000 feathers on specimens of this fowl. Hummingbirds, however, sport more feathers per body area than any other birds. The cock Phoenix fowl of Japan has the longest feathers; tail feathers of nearly 10.7 metres (35 feet) have been documented.

By contrast, the 13-centimetre (5-inch) long naked mole rat of Africa sprouts only a few scattered, thin hairs on its body. The animal spends its life in sandy soil, digging its way to the plant bulbs and roots that make up its diet.

Eyes are another feature that the animal kingdom has developed to remarkable extremes.

In terms of sheer size, the giant squid is the leader. A 17-metre (55-foot) specimen had an eye diameter of nearly 40 centimetres (16 inches). By contrast, the smallest animal that can form what we would describe as a visual image is the copilia, a marine crustacean that is itself no larger than the head of a pin.

The tarsiers, rat-sized insect-eaters which inhabit a number of western Pacific islands, sport some of the largest eyes in proportion to their body size. A human with similarly proportioned visual organs would have eyes about 30 centimetres (1 foot) across. He would also need a powerful pair of appropriately large sunglasses, for the immense size of the tarsier's eyes has evolved to suit a wholly nocturnal lifestyle.

Among the compound eyes of insects, those of the dragonfly have the most facets of any creature. Some species have as many as 30,000 facets in each eye, allowing an almost hemispherical view of the world. By contrast, the eyes of some dark-adapted ants have just nine facets each.

Placement of the eyes gives the rabbit family the greatest field of vision, nearly a full 360 degrees in the common cottontail. Because its eyes are so far apart, the rabbit's blind spot lies directly in front of it.

Such placement allows prey species such as the rabbit constantly to survey as much of their environment as possible, keeping a full-time watch for predators.

Most predators, on the other hand, have their eyes placed directly in the front of their heads, giving them less of a field of vision but much greater depth perception – an essential for pursuing prey.

Take a moment to look into a mirror and you will see that humans' eyes are definitely those of the predator, despite some dimming in the long process of civilization. We have a field of vision of more than 200 degrees, but a frontal overlap of nearly 180 degrees and superior depth of field perception. Cats, another family of predators, have fields of vision in the 180-degree range.

Starfish have the most distinctive placement of eyes, on the ends of their feet, the 'points' of their 'stars.' Rays, sole, and flounders are the only fish with both eyes on one side of the head.

The eyes of chameleons are set atop small 'towers' and can be moved independently of one another, thus allowing the animal to see in two directions at the same time. One eye might be scanning above the animal, while the other is looking straight ahead. Looking through two telescopes, one at each eye, in different directions simultaneously might give us a sense of what the chameleon sees.

An 'eye' of a different sort is that of the lantern-eye fish, any of several small species that inhabit the Pacific and Caribbean oceans. Under each normal eye is a second, eye-like mechanism. Colonies of bioluminescent bacteria live in this structure, under a transparent covering. The bacteria give off light at all times, but the fish controls the situation by drawing a fold of skin over the light when it wants to turn it 'off.'

The dippers, several species of wren-sized birds, use a similar membrane – actually a transparent third eyelid – to protect their eyes and still be able to see while they are underwater. They live in close proximity to mountain streams, in which they spend much of their time swimming in search of food. For a dipper bird entering the water is simply a matter of walking straight into the stream and disappearing below the surface. Although it appears that the bird is now walking on the stream bed, it is actually swimming.

At first consideration, limbs might appear to be one variable with quite limited variability. But when the full range of animal life is brought into the picture, an amazingly complex situation is revealed.

Numbers of limbs vary from the single platform with which a snail propels itself to the record 710 legs counted on one millipede. In between, we find the hoofed animals like deer, which are quadrupeds; the starfish, with 5 legs; ants, beetles, bees and the like, with six; octopi and spiders, 8; shrimp and lobster, 10; the wood louse, 14; caterpillars, 16; pauropods, 18; symphylans, 24; and centipedes, anywhere from 28 to 354.

In this manner, the diversity of body design continues beyond the capacity of any book to record it, limited only by the total number of animal species. Every one of them offers its own variations.

BELOW This two-clawed hunting spider and one of its offspring are typical of spiders, having eight legs.

Defensive Postures

One of the keys to survival for any animal is the ability to avoid, deter or withstand attacks from other animals. Size, as we have already seen, is one factor in this constant struggle. Colouration, as we will see in a later chapter, is another. But some animals have developed extraordinary methods and devices to accomplish the same goals.

Some of them attempt to give the appearance of death in the hope that the threat will pass, leaving them unharmed. The technique is often referred to as 'playing possum', after its most famous example, the Virginia opossum.

When threatened, this marsupial will often feign death by lying on its side, closing its eyes, opening its mouth and dangling its tongue out onto the side of its face. At times the ruse is so complete that breathing is difficult to detect in the animal.

Some people have conjectured that the deathlike state is actually a case of mild shock, rather than any deliberate trickery on the part of what is truly an otherwise rather simple creature. In addition, people having any familiarity with opossums will report that the animal does not react to threats in this manner. At times,

ABOVE *When threatened the opossum generally feigns death. It does this so well that even its breathing is difficult to detect.*

BELOW *If its initial attempt to convince an attacker that it is actually a much more dangerous individual fails, the hognosed snake rolls onto its back and fakes its own death.*

RIGHT *To escape an enemy, the wood turtle simply pulls its head, legs and tail into its armour-like shell.*

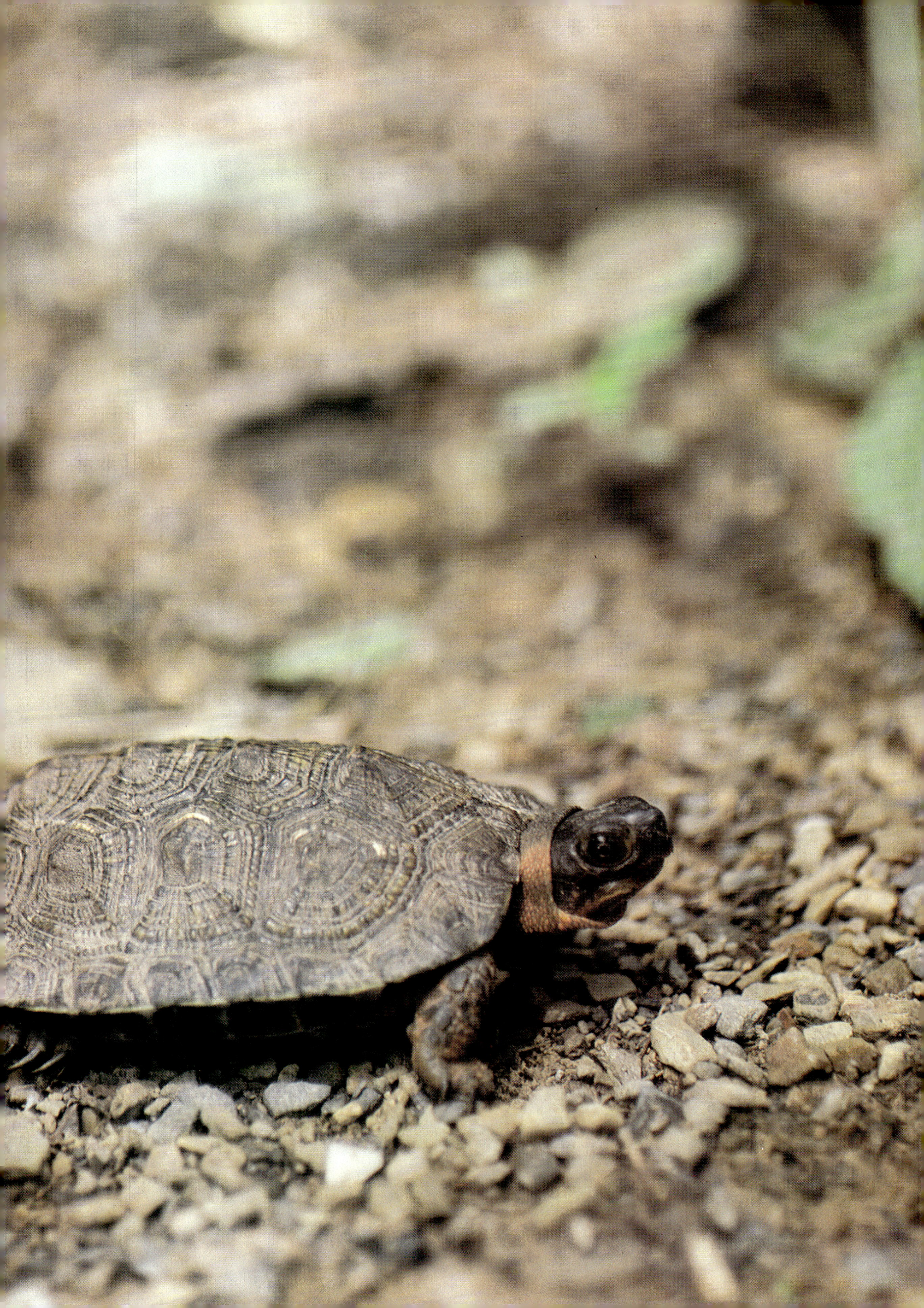

ABOVE The pill bug has earned its name by rolling into a small, pill-like ball, exposing only its jointed shell to attackers.

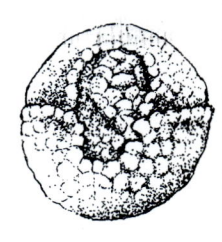

ABOVE The 'armour-plated' armadillo defends itself against attackers by rolling into a tight ball – protecting its vulnerable parts – and feigning death.

an opossum can be a snarling, spitting mass of gray fur.

Feigning death is part of the repertoire of another relatively harmless North American animal, the hognosed snake. The first bluff that the reptile tries to pull on an attacker is to pretend to be a much more dangerous snake. It lifts its long ribs, stretches loose skin over them and fattens the body. Rising a bit off the ground, it has the appearance of some strangely colored cobra. The hognosed snake will hiss, sway from side to side and even strike. It will not, however, open its mouth.

If 'plan A' fails, the snake will roll over onto its back and writhe in its 'last death throes'. Its mouth will drop open and the tongue will roll out. If it is rolled over, it will immediately thrust itself back onto its back.

Some other animals, such as armadillos and turtles, also play dead when threatened, though in a less histrionic way, relying on a natural form of armour.

The body of an armadillo – the largest species of which is Brazil's 57-kilogram (125-pound) giant armadillo – is covered by bony plates that repel most attacks. The armadillo rolls itself into a ball, with only the plates exposed, and waits for the attacker to tire.

Pangolins, a group of scaly anteaters that can weigh as much as 27 kilograms (60 pounds) and of which there are four species in Africa and three in Asia, make use of a similar covering of overlapping scales on its back, legs and tail. The pangolin sleeps in this protected position, in a den, in a hollow tree or wedged into the fork of a tree. A mother pangolin nestles her young to her belly and then envelopes herself around them.

The chiton, a marine mollusc, has eight hinged plates which will bend around its body in the same type of formation. Many of the millipedes carry similar armour, but also rely on foul-tasting or poisonous secretions.

Most turtles simply withdraw all soft body parts into the sanctuary of their shells. Both the top, or carapace, and the bottom, or plastron, generally have an outer layer of horny scales and an inner layer of jointed bones. These two sections are usually joined at the animal's sides by a bony bridge with openings for heads, legs and tail. The plastron is hinged in some species, such as the box turtle, to completely seal the openings when the turtle retreats inside.

Quills and spines substitute for shells and armor in other animals, the most famous of which is the North American porcupine. However, its Old World cousins actually have much longer quills.

The North American species carries about 30,000 3- to 13-centimetre (1- to 5-inch) quills on its back, sides and tail. The quills – actually modified hairs with as many as a thousand barbs each – are attached to loose voluntary muscles.

Although the porcupine prefers to escape danger by retreating up the nearest tree, when defence is its only way out it erects its quills, lowers its heads and slashes with its tail. The animal cannot throw its quills at an attacker, as folklore has it doing time and time again. But when its tail strikes the attacker, the loosely seated quills are driven into that animal.

The body heat of the attacker causes the barbs to expand, which, in concert with involuntary muscle re-actions, drives the quill further into the foe. There have been confirmed reports of a quill piercing the heart of a would-be attacker.

Only a few carnivores have developed an ability to prey regularly on porcupines. The fisher, a large mink-like animal, is skilled at flipping the porcupine onto its back and attacking its quill-less belly. One of the 'signs' listed for the fish in most identification guides is a scat with quills. Nevertheless, fishes do suffer fatal injuries in some of these attacks.

Mating porcupines face some of the same challenges as an attacking fisher. The male must be careful not to approach closely before the female is sufficiently aroused to relax her quills, lift her tail onto her back and present herself.

About seven months later a solitary baby is born. Its fully formed quills do not injure the mother because

TOP *Only a few mammals have external bony plates as their principal means of defence. One is the armadillo.*

ABOVE *Few animal defences can stand up to the modern machinery and devices of man.*

RIGHT *Despite popular myth, the porcupine cannot throw its quills. When threatened, however, it does erect the quills on its back and thrashes at its attacker with its tail. The quills pull free on contact.*

BELOW *The king cobra is the largest poisonous snake, growing to around 5.5 metres (18 feet). If disturbed, the cobra rears up, flattening the skin around the neck area to form the characteristic hood – a posture designed to warn off the unwary. However, should the cobra strike, its venom is extremely toxic – strong enough to fell an elephant or 30 men.*

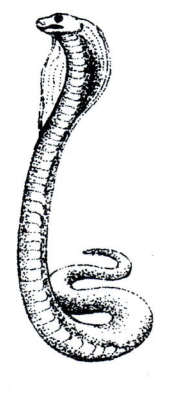

they are soft initially, and the baby is born head first.

The marine porcupine fish earns its apt name by swallowing air or water to inflate itself and cause its spines to protrude when threatened.

The much smaller hedgehog of Europe also has a body covered with short, sharp spines. When threatened, the animal rolls itself into a ball, offering only the uplifted spines to the attacker. The common hedgehog has developed an immunity to the venom of vipers, and actually includes them in its diet.

The moloch, an Australian lizard also known as the thorny devil, has a body completely covered with protective spines. Some describe it as the ugliest lizard in the world. Its diet is equally peculiar, consisting only of ants, as many as a thousand of them at a time.

Hermit crabs are known as the apartment dwellers of the animal kingdom because of their use of other creatures' discards as extra protection for their own shells. Some species, like the grenadier crab, also attach the stinging tentacles of the sea anemone to their commandeered shells. Protection is obviously one of their motivations, but some observers believe there may also be as yet unexplained reasons for the action.

Similarly, the marine mollusc *Glaucus atlanticus* steals the stinging cells from the tentacles of the Portuguese man-of-war. It feeds on the tentacles and somehow, perhaps by chemical reaction, deactivates the stinging cells, digests them whole, incorporates them into its own fingerlike projections, and then reactivates them for use in its own protection.

Many species of jellyfish, such as the man-of-war, have stinging cells called nematocysts in their tentacles. The luminescent sea wasp of the world's tropical and sub-tropical waters is the most venomous. Its toxin can paralyze the heart within minutes.

The sea snake of the coastal waters of northwestern Australia may be the most venomous snake alive. Its venom is estimated to be at least 100 times as toxic as the venom of the taipan, another Australian snake whose venom has killed humans in only a few minutes.

Sea snakes are generally non-aggressive, and only a quarter of those people bitten by them are poisoned. Of those who are poisoned, however, a full quarter die. Symptoms can take several hours to develop.

The king cobra of India, South China and the Philippines (at about 5.5 metres (18 feet) the largest poisonous

DEFENSIVE POSTURES

ABOVE An attacker finds only a ball of sharp spines when it goes after a hedgehog.

snake in the world) generates a venom strong enough to bring down a full-grown elephant, or more than 30 men (the venom of the sea snake has been estimated to be as much as 50 times as lethal). Before striking, the cobra lifts the front of its body and flattens the skin around the neck area into the form of a hood. However, the cobra is actually rather shy and would prefer to rely on its threatening posture to forestall the need for attack.

Many species of cobra can spit venom, but the spitting cobra of Africa has made this action its trademark. It can spit the potent substance on-target as far as 2.14 metres (7 feet), and farther, with greatly reduced accuracy. The snake carries a ready supply of venom to enable six or more ejections in immediate succession. After the supply is exhausted, within less than a day the snake will be ready to spit again.

Landing on skin or fur, the venom is harmless. But it can penetrate cuts and body openings, and is painful in the eyes, even causing blindness.

The mongoose, a weasel-like animal of India, Ceylon and southeast Asia, makes its living in part by destroying snakes including the cobra. Despite popular folklore, the various species of mongoose are not immune to the

ABOVE The hedgehog's spines are well developed when the tiny animal is still quite young.

45

EXTRAORDINARY ANIMALS

TOP *Lacking any armour of its own, the hermit crab borrows the shells of other creatures, discarding and replacing them as it grows or finds more suitable accommodation.*

ABOVE *The Gaboon viper carries the longest fangs of any snake. Individuals have been found dead with their own fangs protruding through the backs of their necks.*

snake's venom. Instead, they rely on their quickness and agility to make the kill, which is usually accomplished by breaking the snake's neck.

The mongoose's diet also includes other reptiles, small mammals, birds and insects. So adept is this small animal at killing rats that in some regions where the two groups live, the rats have taken to the trees, which the mongoose cannot climb.

Among snakes, the longest fangs on record are those of the Gaboon viper of Africa, which may be nearly 5 centimetres (2 inches) long. There have been reports of these snakes accidentally killing themselves by embedding their fangs into their own bodies.

Snakes, however, are far from the only poisonous animals. Many spiders carry venom, the most potent of which probably belongs to the Brazilian wandering spider. When disturbed – as it frequently is because of its penchant for lurking in human clothing and shoes – the large spider bites several times. Human fatalities are few, however, because of the availability of an effective antivenin.

The gila monster and its close relative the Mexican bearded lizard, of southwestern United States and Mexico, are the only poisonous lizards. They carry their poison in glands in their lower jaws, whereas snakes

46

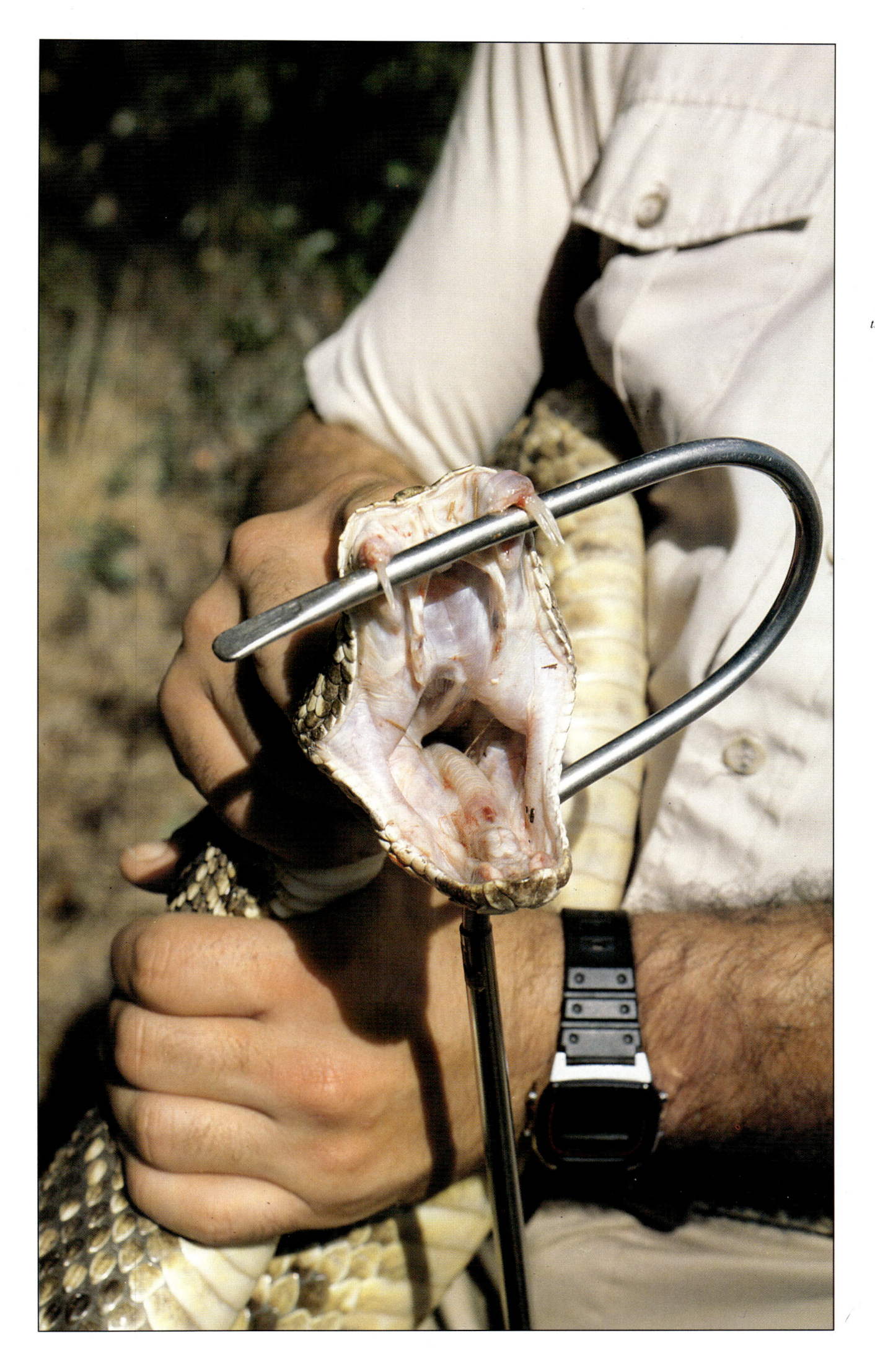

LEFT An experienced handler exposes the business end of a large eastern diamond rattlesnake.

RIGHT One of the few species to eat milkweed leaves, the monarch butterfly absorbs the toxins from the plant, giving it protection from many predators.

DEFENSIVE POSTURES

ABOVE The venomous black widow spider offers its trademark red hour-glass insignia as a warning to would-be intruders.

carry it in upper-jaw glands. These lizards do not have fangs, but their teeth are grooved to deliver the toxin into the wound after it moves along the grooved lower lip. The lizard, therefore, must maintain its grasp on the victim until the venom flows to the wound. The venom is a neurotoxin, which causes death by paralyzing the respiratory mechanism.

Many frogs and toads also produce poison, generally delivered as a secretion through the skin. The most toxic of these is the poison-arrow frogs of Central and South America, which some native tribes use to obtain poison for their arrow tips. These frogs are brightly coloured in combinations of reds and blues with black as a warning to would-be attackers.

The weeverfish family, found off the coasts of Europe, Africa and South America, is probably the most dangerous of the bony fishes. The long, blade-like spines of their dorsal fin can deliver a sting fatal to humans. The sting causes instant, severe pain which grows more intense as the toxin takes effect and reaches a peak within about 30 minutes. At this peak, even morphine often cannot relieve the pain. The pain diminishes in a couple of hours, but is followed by nausea, headache, fever, chills, breathing problems, convulsions and sometimes death.

The jagged spines along the back of the stonefish of Australia or the dorsal fins of many of the 350 different species of zebra fish can likewise cause death within a few hours.

Some octopi also carry potent venom – the most deadly of which is that of the tiny blue-ringed octopus of Australia. The venom can cause respiratory failure within two hours, whereas some attacks have caused temporary paralysis followed by complete recovery.

The milkweed and monarch butterflies acquire their poisoning abilities from the milkweed that forms the

LEFT The bite of the tarantula is rarely fatal to large creatures, including man. However, it is quite effective in stopping the creature's small prey.

49

ABOVE Some species of electric eel can deliver short charges several times greater than the voltage of household electrical current.

RIGHT Although not as powerful as the electric eels, several species of catfish have also developed the ability to delivery short charges of electricity. They use it to stun their prey.

basis of their diet. The milky juices of the milkweed are poisonous, to one degree or another, to most other creatures. But these butterflies thrive on it and pass its poison into their own tissues. Predators who have tasted one of them generally decline future opportunities.

A few mammals can deliver a poison of their own. The male platypus, as we have noted, has sharp, venomous spines on each of his back legs.

Other animals have developed the ability to generate electricity. About 250 species of fish fall into this category, including electric eels. About three-quarters of an electric eel's body is actually an electricity-producing mechanism. Some species have as many as 6,000 electric cells. The 10-foot *Electrophorus electricus* of South American rivers can deliver a charge of 600 volts. By comparison, the voltage of electricity being supplied to homes is generally 240 V or 120 V.

Torpedo rays have developed the same ability. A 1.8 metre (6-foot) *Torpedo nobilianna* of the Atlantic and Mediterranean can discharge 200 volts, enough to stun a

DEFENSIVE POSTURES

ABOVE A skunk will stamp its feet in warning before turning around and letting loose its potent spray.

LEFT The ostrich generally chooses to run from its enemies. But its feet are well equipped for defence, and there have been incidents of the large bird disembowelling humans with one swift kick.

ABOVE Piranha attacks on man are almost completely the creation of movie-makers rather than naturally occurring events. The small fish, however, can strip a large animal to its skeleton in only a few minutes.

man. The muscles at the base of the ray's pectoral fins have been modified to form electrically charged plates, negative below and positive above. After each use of its electric power, the ray must rest and recharge. The first discharge uses most of its stored energy.

Disagreeable odours have become the defence of still other animals, such as the polecat of Europe, the weasel-like zorilla of east Africa and the various skunks of the Americas. When deprived of an escape route or when startled, a skunk can eject a foul-smelling fluid from its anal glands a dozen or more feet. The odour is quite long-lasting, and if the spray is taken directly in the eyes it can cause a very temporary blindness, although it has no long-term detrimental effects. The skunk sprays as its last resort, choosing first to ward-off the threat by stamping its forefeet and raising its tail as a signal.

Some species have no serious defences of their own, but have borrowed the reputation of other more ominous species through mimicking colouration. The milk snakes of North America, for example, bear red, yellow, black and white rings quite similar to those of the poisonous coral snakes.

Still other animals, which normally rely on their powers of flight and escape, can be quite fierce when

RIGHT Lions, like this female over a kill, have been known to attack, kill and eat man. Usually there are very particular circumstances behind such rare incidents.

DEFENSIVE POSTURES

RIGHT *Probably no creature on the face of the earth has received a more unearned reputation for attacks on man than the wolf.*

FAR RIGHT *Many shark attacks, particularly on small boats, have been mistakenly credited to the killer whale.*

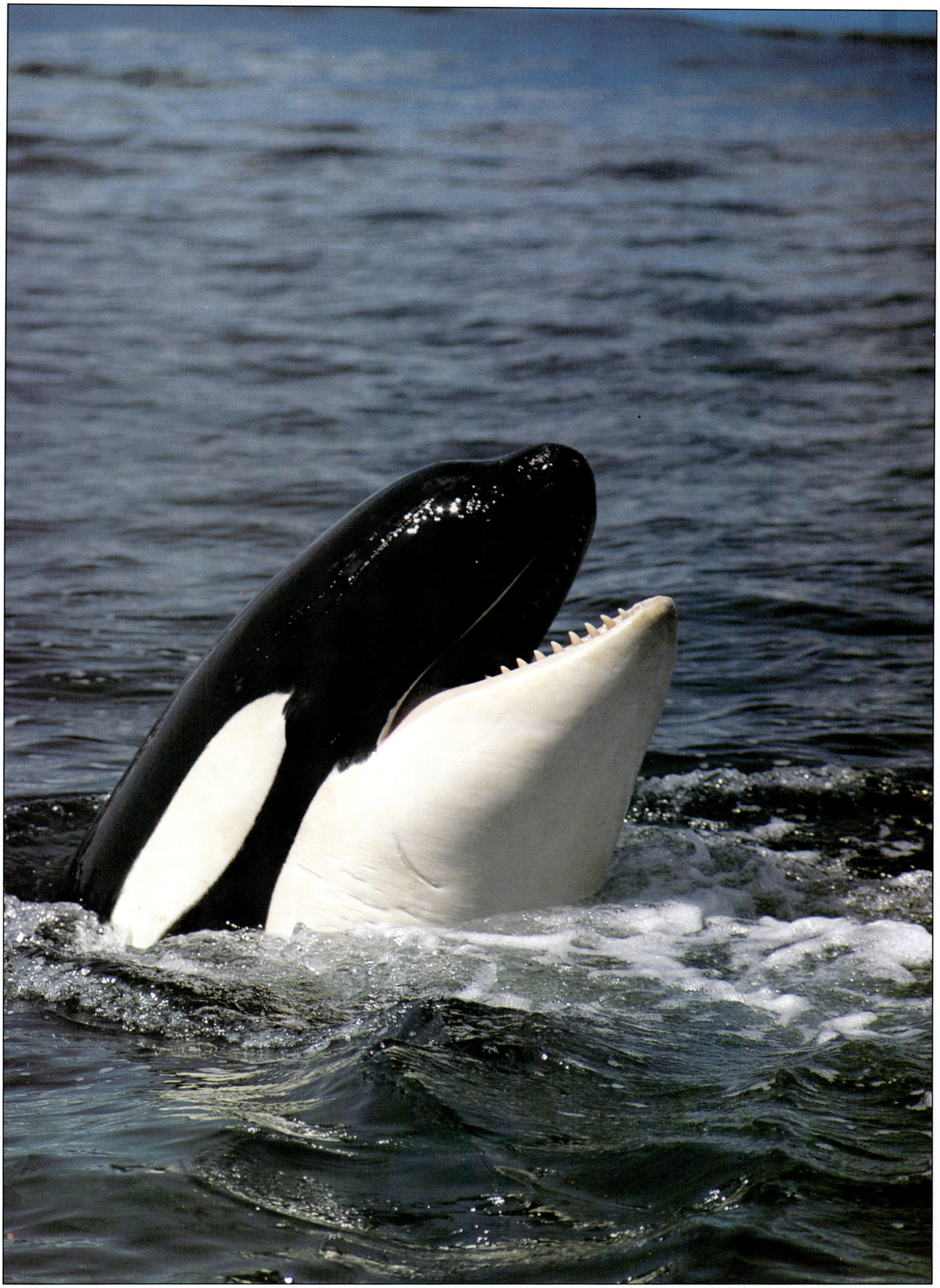

EXTRAORDINARY ANIMALS

ABOVE *Rodents, like this Norway rat, should cause more fear in man than the much larger and more traditionally feared animals. Parasites on the creatures, and the creatures themselves, carry diseases such as "The Plague".*

TOP *The rhino – this one a black rhino – has the equipment to defend itself, but usually opts for a more retiring, shy lifestyle.*

forced into a situation of no alternative but to fight. Ostriches have disembowelled humans with kicks from their powerful, clawed feet. They have also killed humans with kicks to the head.

The red kangaroo of Australia, the largest marsupial, stands up and uses its 9-kilogram (20-pound) tail to support its body, while delivering a dazzling combination of punches and kicks with its arms and legs.

Finally we come to those animals that not only have very strong defences, but also have at times turned their strength or other extraordinary powers directly against man intentionally.

Of the 250 known species of shark, ranging in size from 15 centimetres (6 inches) to possibly more than 18 metres (60 feet), only 39 have registered attacks on human. The most frequent man-biters are the great white, tiger, mako, grey nurse, hammerhead and sand-sharks and the members of the aptly-named requiem family.

The shark is the consummate feeding machine, and has been so for about 100 million years. Its razor-sharp teeth are embedded in the gums in rows, four to 20 deep. The teeth move forward, fall out and are replaced as the shark grows older and when they are used.

The animal can pick up on vibrations 180 metres (200 yards) away, using the nerve endings along its sides from snout to tail. Erratic movements, such as those of a wounded fish or a drowning swimmer, are the most alluring. The shark can also smell a single fluid ounce of fish blood in a million times that amount of water.

Attacks on man by piranha, of which there are more than 20 species in South American rivers, are more the stuff of legend than of truth. However, these small fish certainly have the potential for such devastating attacks. Schools of piranha have been observed to skeletonize a 180-kilogram (400-pound) pig within minutes.

Although most of the wild cats avoid humans, some have been involved in unprovoked attacks on man and in eating human flesh. According to newspaper accounts in the early 1960s, a rampage of man-eating leopards through an Indian district claimed at least 350 lives over a three-year period. Tigers, who have become man-eaters, have sometimes taken to raiding villages for their meals. Lions, generally when pushed by unusual circumstances, have committed dozens of kills over periods of just a few months. By contrast, the mountain lion has had more false accusations levelled at it than any other big cat. Likewise, the jaguar has been accused, but only in unconfirmed reports.

While attacks are somewhat rare, the big cats are among the largest of predators and as such must be considered dangerous. Caution (but not dread or pre-emptive attacks by humans) is always advisable.

The wolf has the most undeserved bad reputation of any animal on earth. Nearly all tales of wolf attacks are quite old and heavily steeped in folklore.

In the bear family, all members have the weapons to attack and easily kill humans, but they generally opt for quick and silent escape instead. The Asian sloth bear commits several attacks each year, some apparently unprovoked. Some accounts of attacks by polar bear appear to tell of unprovoked attacks by bears driven by hunger. The brown bears may attack if provoked or surprised. The black bear generally will not attack, even if provoked.

Killer whales might, very rarely, attack a man, mistaking him for their normal prey of seals and penguins. Many reports of killer whale attacks on boats turn out to be the work of some other large sea-dwelling animal, often the great white shark.

Most elephants will flee at the sight or scent of humans. They have been conditioned to such reaction since birth, feeling the uneasiness that a human's presence generally brings to the herd. Some lone animals have become killers for unknown reasons, and when they do they follow strikingly aberrant behaviour patterns.

Rhinos will charge if provoked, but most of their charges stop short of the object of the attack. These big animals prefer the mock charge as a warning to would-be attackers.

Humans have more to fear from some smaller creatures than from any of those discussed above. Vampire bats in tropical and subtropical America transmit several diseases, including rabies, as they drink the blood of their victims. An estimated million cattle die of bat-carried rabies each year in Latin America, and there are human fatalities as well. Rats (actually parasites on the rats) carried the famous bubonic plague throughout medieval Europe, wiping out the entire populations of some towns. Plague still occurs in much of the developing world. About 60 species of mosquito of the genus *Anopheles* can transmit the causative organisms of human malaria in their bite.

ABOVE Despite the paranoid fear inspired in man by sharks, only 39 of the 250 known species have actually attacked humans; the great white shark, tiger shark and the bull shark having claimed most victims. To put shark attacks in perspective, more people are struck by lightning than are bitten by sharks each year.

LEFT & BELOW Flight is the first option for most creatures, like this gazelle. But when injured or otherwise faced with no options, they will defend themselves.

Special Abilities

Along with the many unusual forms in the animal kingdom come a great many extraordinary abilities.

Speed is one of the most obvious variations among animals, although it is well to remember that speed is affected by the surrounding medium. Flight has obvious advantages over land travel, which, in turn, is generally faster than covering the same distance in water. For our purposes, we will consider all animals on a single scale.

Speeds of nearly 290 kilometres (180 miles) per hour have been reported for the duck hawk, but a documented speed of about 170 kilometres (105 miles) per hour for the spine-tailed swift is probably the fastest that any bird can fly under its own power. Therefore, this small, East Asian bird is the fastest animal. So adapted to life in the air is the swift that it often flies an entire night without a single stop for rest and may even mate on the wing.

On land the cheetah is the undisputed leader, having clocked speeds of as much as 113 kilometres (70 miles) per hour over very short distances. This African cat also has amazing powers of acceleration; it can reach 64 kilometres (40 miles) per hour within two seconds. However the cheetah can maintain its speed for only short distances, after which it must stop for rest. Compared to the cheetah, humans are slow: a man can run an average 32 kilometres (20 miles) per hour.

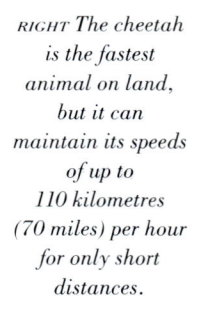

RIGHT *The cheetah is the fastest animal on land, but it can maintain its speeds of up to 110 kilometres (70 miles) per hour for only short distances.*

RIGHT *This black-tailed rattlesnake, like other pit vipers, can locate prey in total darkness using the heat-sensing organs on both sides of its face.*

58

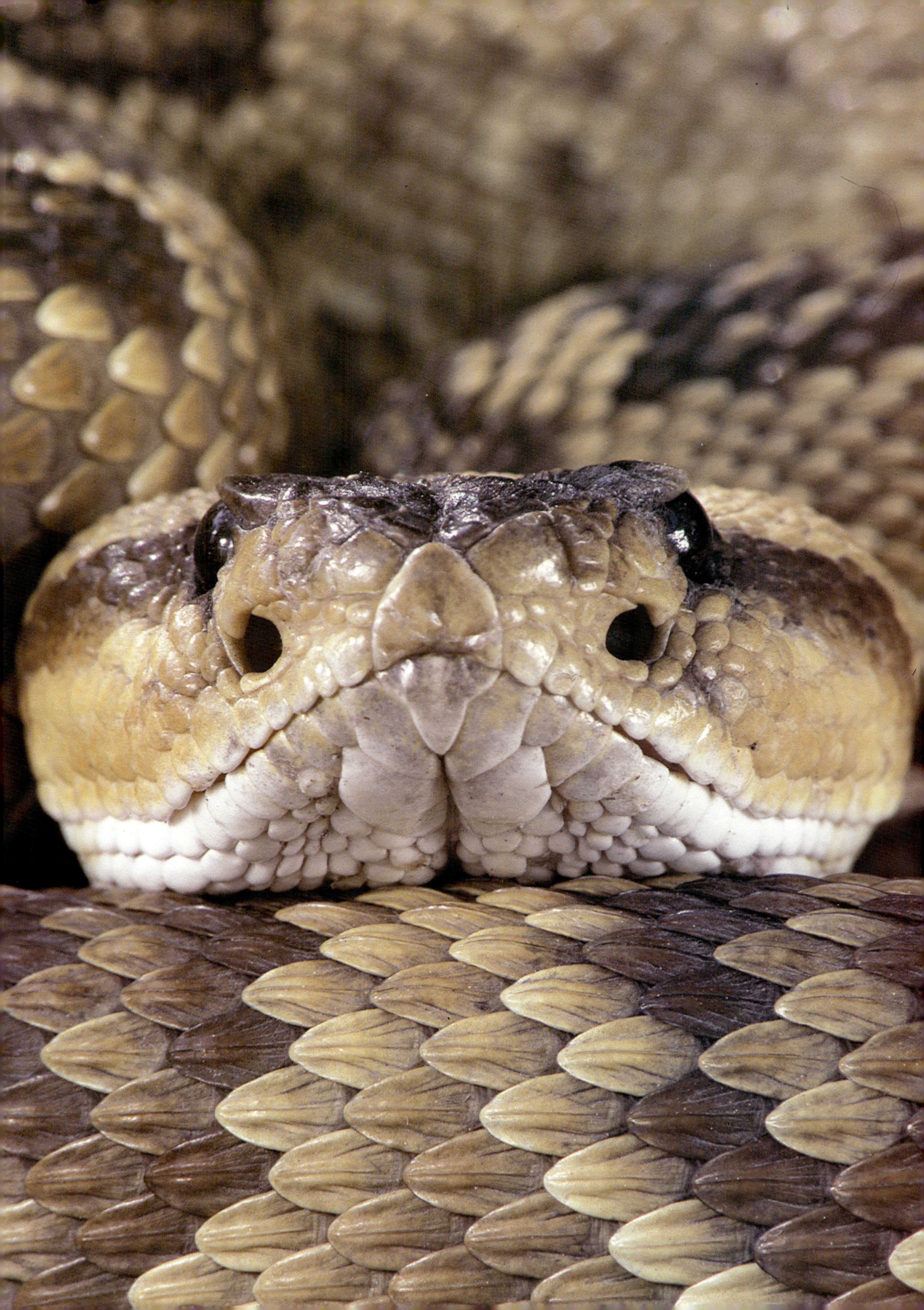

EXTRAORDINARY ANIMALS

RIGHT *Able to move about easily through its tree-home, the three-toed sloth can only pull its great weight along with its front-legs when on the ground. It is thus among the slowest of all animals.*

The three-toed sloth of South America is the slowest of all mammals. Able to move easily about its arboreal home, the animal is nearly helpless on the ground, dragging itself along by its front feet and legs at only about 1.8 to 2.5 metres (6 to 8 feet) per minute.

The sailfish is the speedster of the water, able to flash along at speeds greater than 95 kilometres (60 miles) per hour. A human swimmer moves through the water at about 8.5 kilometres (5¼) miles per hour.

These are average speeds. An individual humming-bird, for example, with its wings vibrating at 200 beats per second in full flight, might exceed 48 kilometres (30 miles) per hour. That, of course, would be for flying straight ahead. These tiny birds are also capable of flying backwards, up and down, and hovering.

Likewise, the fastest bats – the noctule and long-winged species – have both been clocked at a full 50 kilometres (31 miles) per hour across open areas.

Although the word 'flying' is used in the names of many non-avian species, the bat is the only non-bird animal capable of actual flight. Among the 2,000 or so species worldwide, the bat with the largest wingspan is

SPECIAL ABILITIES

SPEED COMPARISON

SPINE-TAILED SWIFT	105 MPH
PIGEON	60 MPH
DRAGONFLY	50 MPH
OWL	40 MPH
HAWK MOTH	34 MPH
HUMMING BIRD	30 MPH
AMERICAN ROBIN	30 MPH
BAT	15 MPH
HONEYBEE	10 MPH
HOUSE FLY	5 MPH

CHEETAH	70 MPH
PRONGHORN ANTELOPE	60 MPH
GAZELLE	50 MPH
JACK RABBIT	45 MPH
RACE HORSE WITH RIDER	45 MPH
OSTRICH	40 MPH
GREY FOX	40 MPH
GREYHOUND	40 MPH
HOUSE CAT	30 MPH
ELEPHANT	25 MPH
MAN	20 MPH
SNAKE	2 MPH
THREE-TOED SLOTH	1 MPH
BOX TURTLE	1/10 MPH

SAILFISH	60 MPH
BLUEFIN TUNA	40 MPH
FLYING FISH	40 MPH
DOLPHIN	37 MPH
BARRACUDA	30 MPH
SEA TURTLE	20 MPH
BLUE WHALE	20 MPH
TROUT	15 MPH
MAN	5 MPH

BELOW In flight the wings of the honeybee are only a blur to the human eye, as the insect propels itself at speeds of up to 16 kilometres (10 miles) per hour.

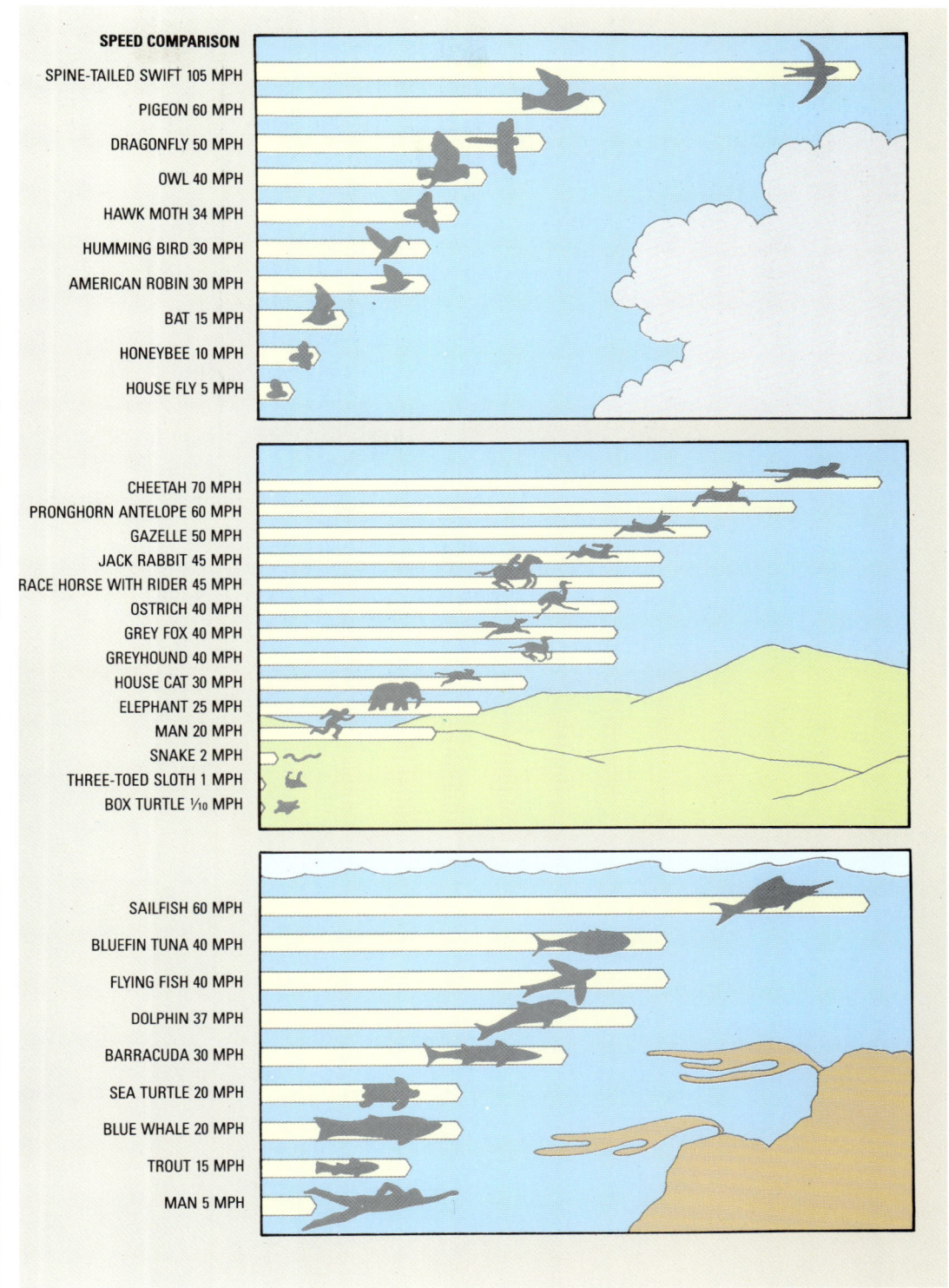

the kalong, a fruit bat of Malaysia and Indonesia. Its span can be as much as 1.7 metres (5 feet 7 inches), whereas the bat's body generally is about 40 centimetres (16 inches) long. The smallest bat, Kitti's hog-nosed of southern Thailand, has a wingspan of about 15 centimetres (6 inches) and a body length of just 4 centimetres (1½ inches).

The other non-avian flyers, could more aptly be called gliders. The flying lemur of Madagascar, for example, can glide for several hundred metres (yards) from one tree to another. However, its gliding membrane, which stretches between its neck and front feet, its front and hind feet, and its hind feet and tip of tail, does not enable it to fly under its own power.

The small 'flying dragon' of southeast Asia glides on

loose folds of skin, held stiff when the lizard lifts its six or seven elongated ribs. The scales on the lizard's body are gray, brown or black, but the 'wings' are bright yellow or orange.

Swimming at speeds of up to 65 kilometres (40 miles) per hour, the flying fish erupts through the surface of the water, stretches its enlarged pectoral fins and glides. Normally, this native of most of the world's warmer seas skims the surface, but it might be 3 metres (10 feet) above the trough between two waves in a rough sea. The fish usually stays aloft for less than a minute, covering as much as 0.4 kilometre (1¼ mile) in that time.

When we turn to movement through the ocean's depths, we find that the sperm whale is the deepest diver. This whale can descend more than 3,000 metres (10,000 feet) in pursuit of food, and is able to stay down for nearly two hours. The only other marine mammals to dive more than 900 metres (3,000 feet) are the killer whale, the bottle-nosed whale and the Berardius.

The massive blue whale can dive to about 460 metres

ANIMAL DIVING ABILITY COMPARISON TABLE

1 MAN 280 FT
2 MAN WITH SCUBA GEAR 440 FT
3 HARP SEAL 900 FT
4 BLUE WHALE 1500 FT
5 WEDDELL SEAL 1968 FT
6 MAN IN DEEP DIVING SUIT 2000 FT
7 KILLER WHALE 4000 FT
8 SPERM WHALE 10000 FT
9 BATHYSCAPHE SMALL DEEP DIVING SUBMARINE 35802 FT

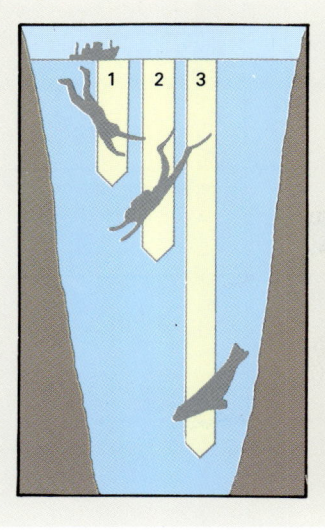

LEFT *Many species of snakes, like this eastern garter snake in Quebec, crawl along quite slowly, making them prime photo subjects for the non-squeamish.*

LEFT The many species of bats worldwide are the only non-bird animals capable of true flight.

(1,500 feet), but its huge lungs – which might weigh more than a ton – enable it to stay underwater for more than two hours. When it finally surfaces, it might exhale, or blow, for as long as five minutes to ready its lungs for another breath of fresh air.

The Weddell seal, which is the world's most southerly living mammal, has made the deepest dive ever recorded for a pinniped. This seal, which lives along Antarctica, has been down as far as 600 metres (1968) feet and has stayed down for 43 minutes. Next best was probably a harp seal caught in a net at 275 metres (900 feet).

Like most of these abilities, jumping and leaping ability is relative to the size of the animal. The flea might leap 33 centimetres (13 inches), the frog 5.5 metres (18 feet), a man, just over 9 metres (29 feet) and the red kangaroo, more than 12 metres (40 feet). The mountain lion has the greatest leaping range among the cats, reported to be as far as 12 metres (40 feet). The jack rabbit, which is actually a hare rather than a true rabbit, can manage 7.6 metres (25 feet) horizontally and 2,4 metres (8 feet) vertically. But the vertical winner must be the klipspringer, a 9-kilogram (20-pound) African antelope that can jump 7.6 metres (25 feet) vertically. This animal can also land securely on a very small spot.

ANIMAL JUMPING/ LEAPING COMPARISON TABLE

In general, jumping and leaping ability is relative to the size of the animal. However, animals with especially strong hind leg or lower limb development, such as the examples shown here, can leap astonishing distances in relation to their size.

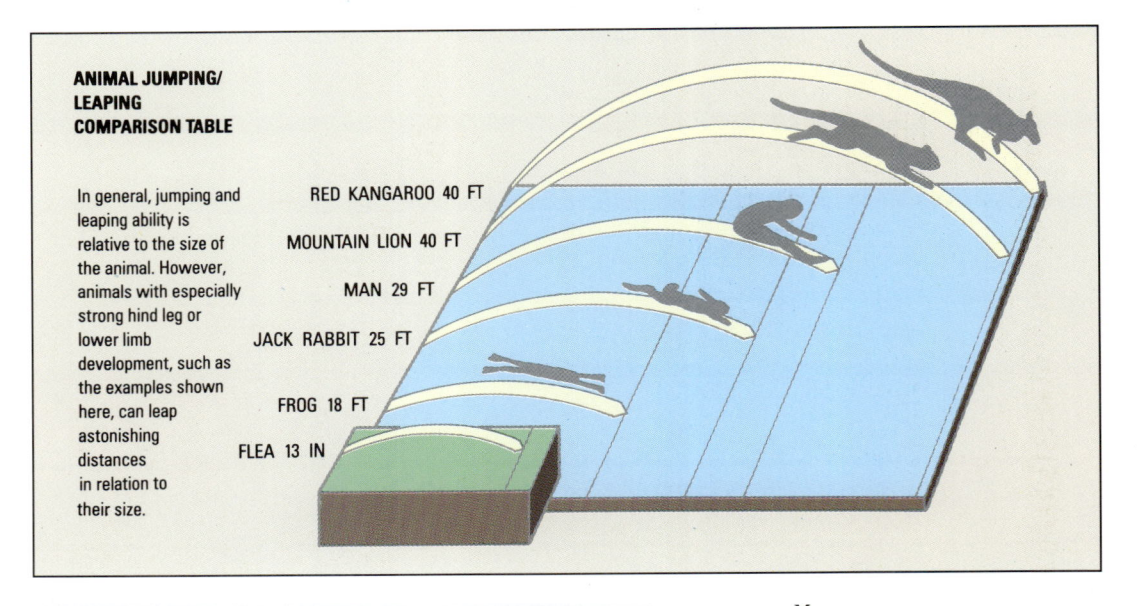

RED KANGAROO 40 FT
MOUNTAIN LION 40 FT
MAN 29 FT
JACK RABBIT 25 FT
FROG 18 FT
FLEA 13 IN

LEFT Many "flying" animals, like this flying squirrel, actually glide from one position to the next on flaps of skin.

ABOVE The terrestrial snail is among the slowest creatures alive.

RIGHT *With recorded leaps of 12 metres (40 feet), the mountain lion or cougar may hold the animal-record in this category.*

HAWKS EYESIGHT

A bird of prey's eyesight is vastly superior to man's. Flying at a height at which, say a gyrfalcon, would be indiscernable to the eye of a person, the same gyrfalcon is thought to be able to see in detail its prey, a pair of pigeons for example, on the ground.

Animals' senses, as well as their feats of locomotion, can astonish us. Some birds of prey are said to be able to see detail in a prey animal, such as a rabbit, from so high in the air that the bird itself would be invisible to a person on the ground.

Many animals also display astounding night vision. The eyes of cats, including the common house cat, are eight times more sensitive to light than man's. The common toad's eyes have this same power.

Some snakes make use of two types of sight, being able to pick up on infrared radiation with special organs and thus receive a heat picture of their prey. The boids, such as the boa constrictor, python and anaconda, have rows of as many as 13 heat-sensitive organs. The pit vipers, such as the rattlesnakes and moccasins, have the organs on both sides of their face between their eyes and nostrils.

These organs can detect changes of much less than a degree of temperature and deliver a response within 35 milliseconds. The same area of the snake's brain that interprets signals from the eyes works on signals from the heat organs. The heat-produced image is of much lower resolution, but detailed enough to reveal warm-blooded prey to the snake.

As a defence against such specialized hunting devices, the kangaroo rat of North America's arid regions has developed such large eardrums and middle ear chambers that it can pick up on the sound of the rattlesnake's scales sliding across the sand. Whereas the human ear magnifies sound 18 times, the rat's produces amplification of 100.

RIGHT The jackrabbit, like this member of the blacktail species, can jump 8 metres (25 feet).

LEFT This red-tailed hawk has spotted a prey animal in the field below and launched itself from its perch.

LEFT A red-shouldered hawk snatches a snake from the ground in Everglades National Park, Florida.

Many animals' hearing ranges extend far beyond man's extremes of 15 and 20,000 hertz in both directions. One hertz (Hz) equals one cycle per second. The elephant can pick up frequencies as low as 5 Hz. Pigeons can hear even lower. Mice can hear as high as 100,000 Hz, bats up to 200,000 Hz, and the noctuid moth picks up a range from 1,000 to 240,000 Hz.

Elephants communicate primarily with an infrasound just below the range of human hearing. And fin whales use very loud calls at about 20 Hz to communicate across vast stretches of open ocean.

LEFT Elephants can hear sounds of much lower frequency than man. Part of their communication system includes sounds inaudible to us.

SPECIAL ABILITIES

RIGHT *Fireflies produce their yellow glow through bioluminesce, an enzyme mechanism.*

BELOW *Some bats hunt by sight. Others use "bounced" sound in a radar-like manner to locate their prey and other objects.*

Dolphins and some bats use 'bounced' sound to hunt. As the bat cruises, scanning the area, it sends out pulses at about 10 to 20 per second. If it detects an object from returning pulses, it improves its definition to 25 to 50 per second, and as it dives for the kill it might increase the pulse to more than 200 per second. This winged mammal also uses different wavelengths, which bounce off objects differently, to determine fine detail.

A familiar, yet seemingly mysterious phenomenon is the bright yellow flash of the firefly on a warm summer night. This glow is produced by a process known as bioluminescence, which involves an enzyme system that gives off light when exposed to oxygen. This efficient process converts 90 percent of the energy used into light, whereas the average light bulb manages to convert only 10 percent into light.

The firefly makes use of the light in mating, but other creatures have developed similar ability to different ends. The marine hatchet fish carries its lights on its underside and can adjust the intensity to match exactly the light filtering down through the water from the surface, thus making itself virtually invisible from below. The deep sea angler fish dangles its luminous lure on a rod sticking out from its head and quickly gulps anything that takes the bait.

The little archerfish of southeast Asia has developed a sort of 'water-pistol' method of taking its meals. The fish swims near the surface of the water, watching for insects on branches overhead. When it sights a potential morsel, the fish knocks it into the water by spitting water drops at it. The aim is accurate up to 1.2 metres (4 feet).

The Next Generation

Among an animal's principal motivations is the drive to reproduce itself. This urge lies behind the constant battling of bull elk to control the harem of cows – fighting so intense that it uses up some of the fat stores in their bodies, required for survival through the coming winter. It lies behind the roseate bloom on the male breasts of some species of tern, produced by an oil gland only during the mating season.

Without this mechanism drive, the variation in form and function among animals would have little true purpose. What is the point of gaining a competitive advantage through a new development, if no new generations come along to benefit from it. As a matter of fact, uncounted mutations that failed to be passed along have come and gone since the beginning of life.

As reproduction is one of the inherent purposes behind the amazing diversity of the animal kingdom, so, too, this function is itself amazingly varied.

The strange looking platypus, along with the spiny anteaters of Australia and New Guinea, are without peers in the category of odd reproductive methods. Despite the fact that they are members of the same mammalian class of animals as man, dogs, and cattle, for example, they reproduce by laying eggs, like a chicken or a lizard.

BELOW During the autumn rutting season, bull elk battle constantly to maintain their harems of cow elk for mating. They often spend more time keeping the cows close together than actually fighting off other bulls.

RIGHT At just 13 days, the Virginia opossum's pregnancy is the shortest among all animals.

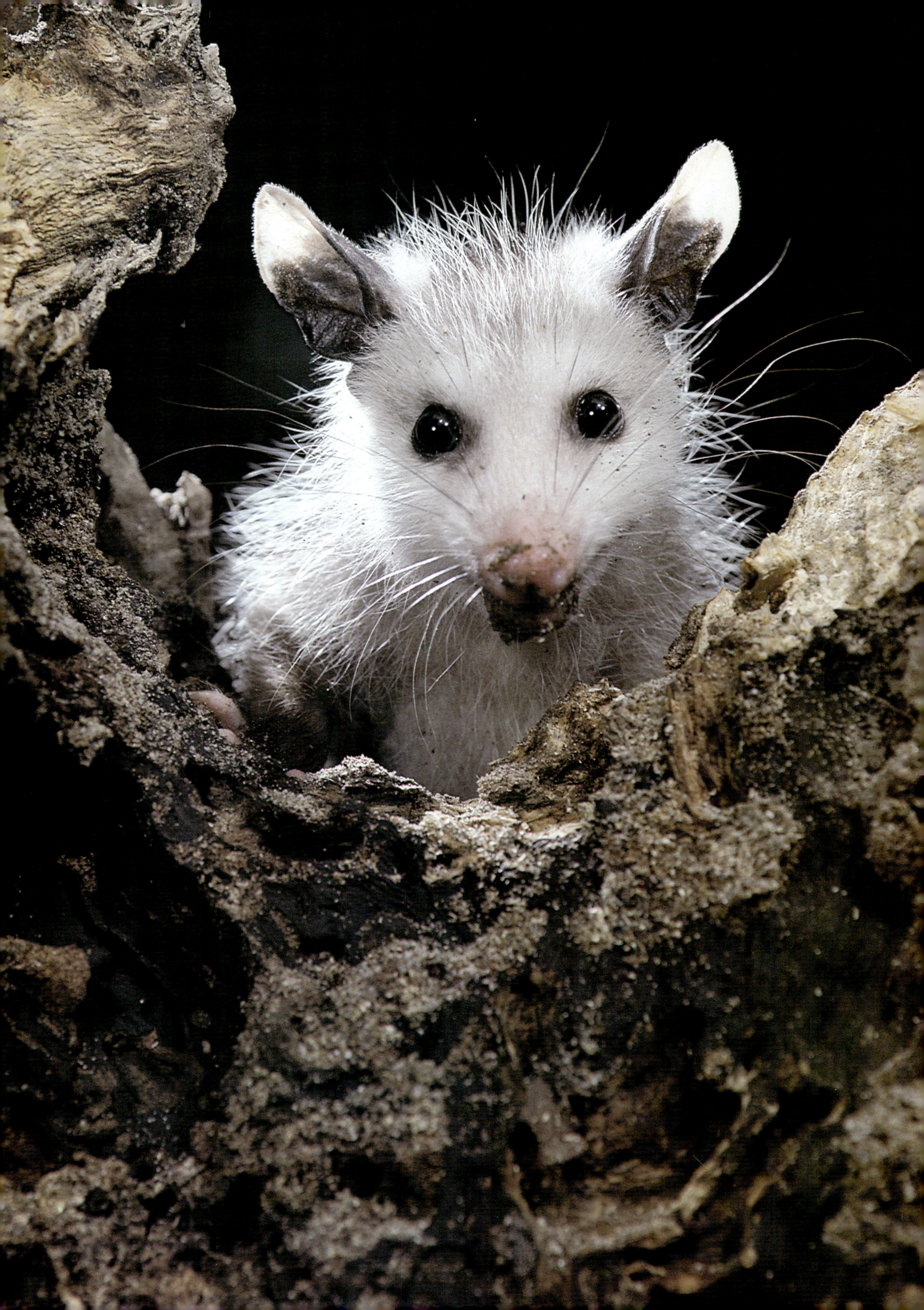

RIGHT *The female sea horse deposits her eggs into the pouch of the male. He then incubates the eggs until they hatch and watches over the brood for their first few days of life.*

FAR RIGHT *A brown thrasher sits on its nest of eggs in a fence row.*

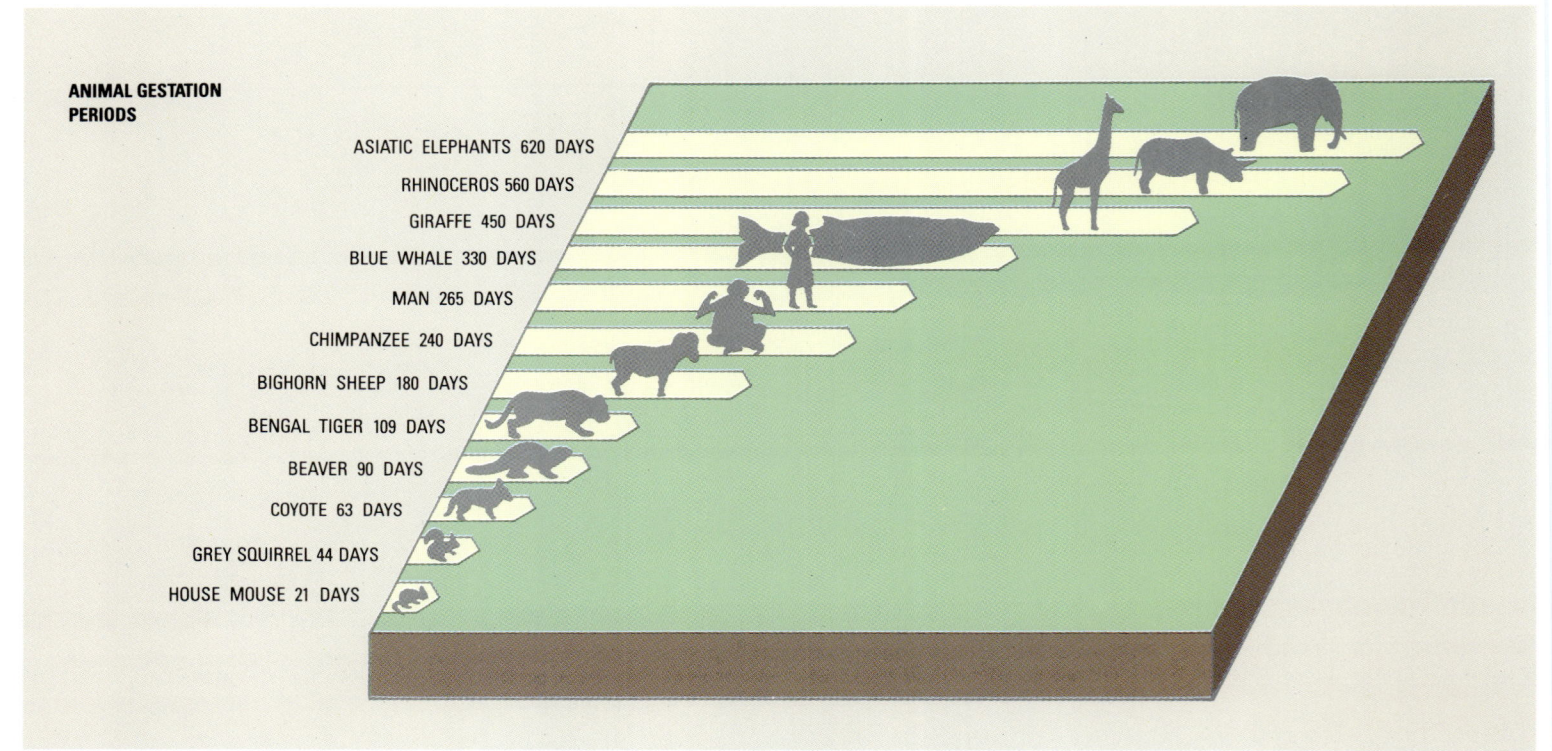

ANIMAL GESTATION PERIODS

- ASIATIC ELEPHANTS 620 DAYS
- RHINOCEROS 560 DAYS
- GIRAFFE 450 DAYS
- BLUE WHALE 330 DAYS
- MAN 265 DAYS
- CHIMPANZEE 240 DAYS
- BIGHORN SHEEP 180 DAYS
- BENGAL TIGER 109 DAYS
- BEAVER 90 DAYS
- COYOTE 63 DAYS
- GREY SQUIRREL 44 DAYS
- HOUSE MOUSE 21 DAYS

The aquatic platypus also employs a rather unusual attractor in its mating ritual, which is initiated by the female. As she swims around the male, occasionally rubbing flanks with him, she eventually vomits a dirty cloud into the water. The male then swims through this cloud and clamps his 'beak' onto her beaverlike tail. After the female tows him about the water for a bit, they will mate.

When fertilized, the platypus egg is about the size of a pea. As it moves through the oviduct, it begins to grow. This is in marked contrast to the eggs of reptiles and birds, which do not increase in size between fertilization and deposit in the nest.

After mating, the female crawls to the back of a burrow she dug earlier in the stream bank, as deep as 18 metres (60 feet), and lays her eggs, two at a time. She coils her body around the eggs to incubate them, and 14 days later the tiny, hairless babies hatch.

The monotremes (as these egg-laying mammals are classified) lack the nipples that are the normal outward sign of the milk-producing organs in mammals. Nevertheless, it is milk that sustains their offspring during their early days.

Platypus milk is secreted onto the skin from glands on the mother's stomach. There the babies lap it up. The echidna (spiny anteater) has a pouch, into which the female places her eggs after laying them. After hatching, the young animals squirm around the inside of the pouch until it finds one of the patches of skin that exude milk.

When the spines of the young echidna become large and sharp enough to begin annoying the tender inside of the pouch, the female will deposit the offspring in a small burrow. She returns every day to nurse it.

Another pouched animal, the Virginia opossum (most commonly referred to as the 'possum') of North America has the shortest pregnancy of any mammal. On average, 13 days after the female becomes pregnant, as many as 20 honeybee-sized young are born.

ABOVE A nestling red-winged blackbird calls out to be fed by its parents.

EXTRAORDINARY ANIMALS

RIGHT *A young New Guinea native displays an ostrich egg, which is the largest egg laid by any living bird.*

74

At this point in our discussion it might serve us well to consider a range of average gestation rates:
Indian elephant, **620** days
rhinoceros, **560**
giraffe, **450**
blue whale, **330**
man, **265**
chimpanzee, **240**
bighorn sheep, **180**
Bengal tiger, **109**
beaver, **90**
coyote, **63**
grey squirrel, **44**
house mouse, **21**
hamster, **16**

Some average incubation rates:
royal albatross, **80** days
cobra, **65**
emperor penguin, **62**
loggerhead turtle, **60**
ostrich, **40**
bald eagle, **35**
great blue heron, **28**
ring-necked pheasant, **22**
ruby-throated hummingbird, **14**
finch, **12**
American toad, **4–12**
Atlantic mackerel, **5**

BELOW *The male ostrich mates with several females, which lay eggs in the same communal nest. All the birds take their turns at incubating the eggs.*

At this point our newborn opossum litter are still very much in the embryonic stage and face another 10 weeks of development before achieving the same level as most mammals at birth. The shortest gestation period for any mammal that delivers fully developed young, is 15 to 16 days for the golden hamster of Syria.

The infant opossums – naked and blind – wiggle their way along a slimy track on the mother's skin, where they attach their mouths to the female's teats and begin the next stage of their development. The female has only 13 teats, so if there are more babies, the unlucky ones that don't find theirs before all feeding stations are taken will soon die.

This seems cruel until one considers that the opossum is already a very prolific animal. If this self-selection process were not functioning the population would quickly outdistance any other natural controls on it, creating catastrophe for the opossums and many other occupants of its widespread habitat.

The young are unable to suck when they first reach the teats, so the mother forces the milk into their mouths by contracting certain muscles. By two months, when they are more fully developed, they can move around inside the pouch and suckle normally. As they mature, they will venture outside the pouch, often riding on their mother's back.

Among sea horses and pipefish, it is the male who has the pouch. The female lays her 200 or so eggs into this brood pouch on the male's belly, where he immediately fertilizes them. He then carries them for 40 to 50 days, until the miniature replicas hatch. For a few days the hatchlings will continue to use the pouch as a refuge.

Similarly, it is the male midwife toad that carries the fertilized eggs after the mating. The eggs are wrapped around his legs, and he returns to water regularly to moisten them.

The female tinamou, a partridge-like bird of Central and South America, also has a detached role in the rearing of the young. She travels from one male to the next, leaving a clutch of eggs for each one to tend. This apparently cavalier attitude is more often adopted by the male in many of the species in which only one of the parents is involved with the offspring.

Among the deep sea angler fish, it is the male that 'disappears', in a manner of speaking, but in an act of extraordinary self-effacement. When he finds a female he attaches himself to her and gradually degenerates into nothing more than a sack of reproductive tissue. He

ABOVE Rhino mating ranges from rough attacks on each other to gentle, tender moments.

draws his life from the female and serves the sole purpose of fertilizing the eggs.

The male ostrich, the largest living bird, takes a much more active role in producing the next generation. He mates with several hens – usually three, but as many as five – which then deposit their eggs into a common nest which he has hollowed out in the sand. For the next 40 days, one of the hens incubates the eggs during the day and the cock takes over the duties for the night.

As might be expected of the earth's largest bird, the ostrich lays the largest egg. Each of the 15 to 30 eggs that a hen produces weigh 1 to 15 kilograms (2 to 3) pounds.

However, the smallest bird – the bee hummingbird of Cuba – does not lay the smallest egg. The Vervain hummingbird of Jamaica lays eggs that weigh slightly more than 0.3 gram ($1/100$ of an ounce), while those of the bee hummingbird generally weigh about twice as much.

In startling contrast to the courtship flights of these tiny birds, with their delicate and gentle nature, is the courtship dance of the rhinoceros, parts of which are very violent. At times, the dance may include attacks on the male by the female. A charging 2,700-kilogram (6,000-pound) rhino – even in the cause of love – is something that one would not soon forget.

However, the courtship also includes a great deal of gentle nuzzling and tenderness. This reflects the great beast's true nature, which generally tends more toward timidity than aggression, except when threatened.

The copulation that follows results in the birth of one offspring 15 to 18 months later. The calf may stay with the mother for as long as two-and-a-half years, and females with one nearly grown calf and another much smaller one have been noted.

Small numbers are common in the offspring of the larger, higher order animals. Man, the apes, elephants, whales and many other species normally produce one offspring at a time.

Lower animals, on the other hand, generally tend towards more offspring more often. For example, the largest litter ever recorded for any wild mammal was 32 at a single birth by a common tenrec, a hedgehog-like insectivore of Madagascar. Not all of the young survived, however. The average litter size for a tenrec is 13 to 14.

A close cousin, the streaked tenrec of the same island, is the youngest breeder among the mammals, being weaned at the age of five days. The female is capable of breeding a mere four weeks after her own birth.

The meadow mouse is the most prolific breeder of all mammals. Some females have produced 17 litters per year, each litter consisting of four to nine babies.

Further down the evolutionary scale we find even more prolific animals, such as the ocean sunfish, which can produce as many as 300 million eggs in one spawning. The edible mussel produces as many as 25 million eggs at a time. The blue crab can generate a clutch of nearly 2 million. One queen termite can produce more than 8,000 eggs per day.

As with most 'rules' about the animal kingdom, however, this one does not always run true. Some species of oceanic ray, for example, lay only two large eggs. The small potter wasp deposits just one egg in the clay pot she created and supplied with a paralyzed caterpillar as food for her future larvae.

The green turtle, a sea turtle of the middle Atlantic and Pacific oceans, might lay her eggs seven times a year, 100 eggs each time, achieving a lifetime total of 1,800 eggs. However, on average, only three of her offspring will live long enough to breed. More than three-quarters of the eggs will never hatch, and nearly all of the hatchlings that do leave the shell will be killed or die of other causes soon thereafter.

The brown bear female generally produces a litter of just two to four cubs, but her success rate is phenomenal compared to that of the green turtle. The cubs stay with her through two winters. When she then enters oestrus again, she will drive them off. If she does not mate, however, they may den together yet another winter.

As the young bears mature, they go through one of the most massive weight gains of all animals. In their first month of life they weigh less than 0.5 kilograms (1 pound) each. As adults they might easily weigh more than 1,000 times as much.

For speed of growth, however, the blue whale is the champion. Starting out as a ovum that is barely visible and weighs far less than an ounce, the calf will grow to 29 tons two years later. Eventually, as an adult, it may reach a length of 30 metres (100 feet) and weigh as much as 125 tons.

The slowest growth rate belongs to the a deep-sea clam of the northern Atlantic Ocean (*Tindaria callistiformis*). Estimates place its growth at less than 8 millimetres (⅓ inch) over a century.

The mating habits of many animals have long fascinated humans; and as one of the most fascinating, the tiger has attracted some unwelcome and harmful attention. Among tigers, copulation is necessary to stimulate the female into ovulation (such animals are called 'induced ovulators'). Therefore, a courting pair of these magnificent big cats may copulate more than 20 times a day while the female is in oestrus.

Unfortunately this biologically necessary behaviour has given the tiger a reputation for lasciviousness that makes it a prize ingredient in some Oriental folk remedies. The penis is held to be one of the strongest of all aphrodisiacs. The loss of its habitat is a much greater threat to the tiger than slaughter to serve such worn-out beliefs, but illegal hunting does occur.

The tiger averages two to four cubs in a litter, as does the next largest cat, the lion. But the largest recorded litter for one of the big cats was seven cubs born to a lioness at the Dublin Zoo in the mid-1960s.

ABOVE *Brown bear cubs may stay with their mother through three winters before she again enters oestrus and drives them off.*

All the Colours of the Rainbow

The natural processes that have produced the variations already discussed have had an equally evident impact on the colouration of the animal kingdom. For camouflage and disguise, for mating and reproduction, for warning and mimicry, one animal or another has taken on every colour of the rainbow, every combination and every blend.

Some have developed the use of different colours and patterns at different stages of their lives, different situations in their daily lives and each of the different seasons of the year.

The chameleons have the most universally known reputation for quick colour change. There is no disputing that their various shades of brown and green certainly do allow them to match their environment quite closely at times. These small reptiles achieve even more striking changes when displaying for defensive, territorial or courtship reasons.

However the most rapid colour changes in the entire animal world are accomplished by the cuttlefish, octopi and squid. Some of these species can effect a complete change in less than a second, utilizing specialized chromatophore cells which contain various colour pigments.

RIGHT The chameleon, a general description for several dozen different species of reptile, is probably the most famous of earth's colour-changers, although several other animals perform the feat much faster.

RIGHT Several species of butterfly have developed colouring similar to the monarch, although they do not have the poisonous character of their mimicked object.

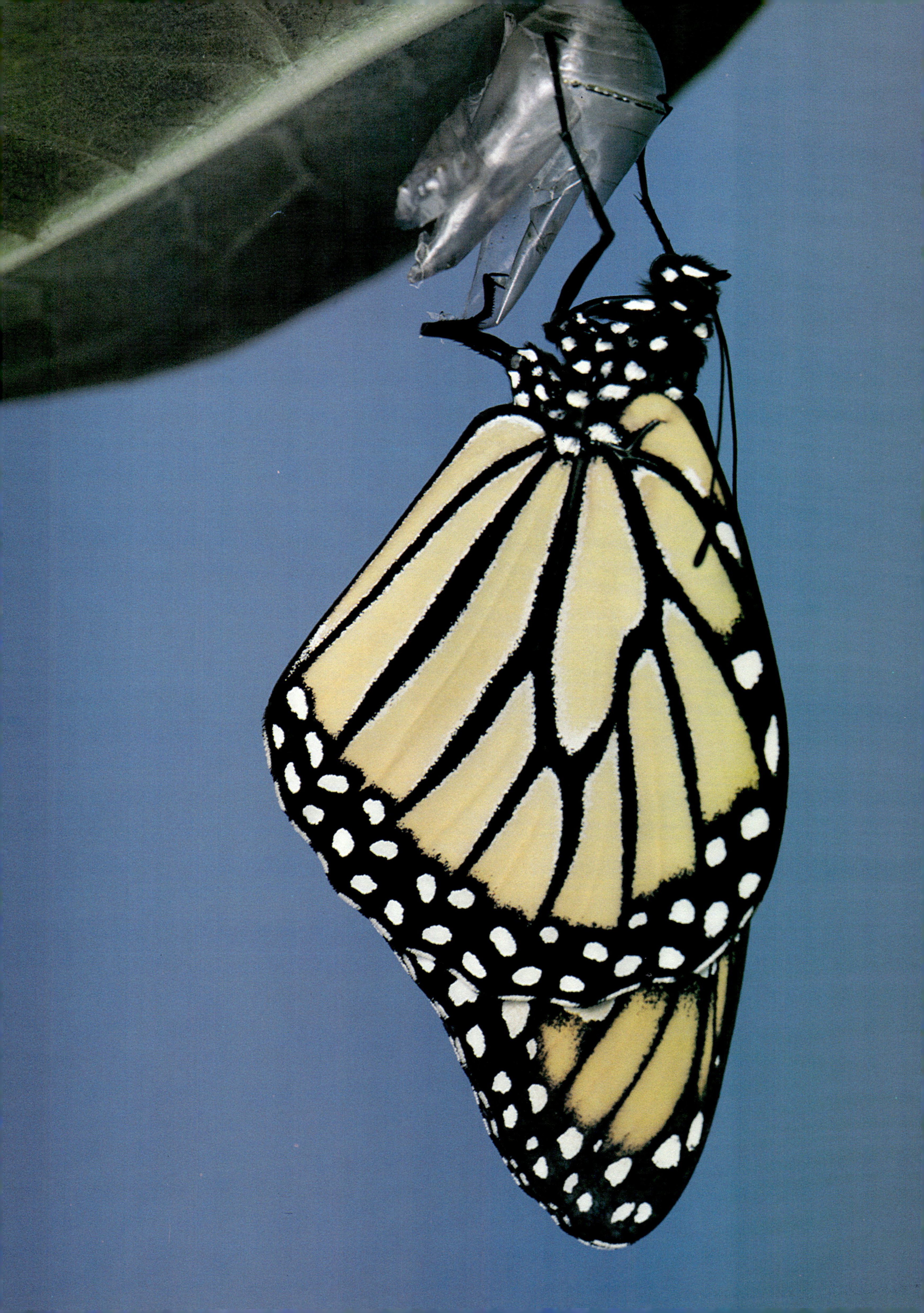

EXTRAORDINARY ANIMALS

RIGHT *The spotted coat of the white-tailed deer fawn makes for excellent camouflage in the sun-spotted, forest world of the animal.*

BELOW *The winter coat of a snowshoe hare helps the animal to blend into its snow-covered environment.*

When the animal contracts the appropriate muscle, the elastic membrane that encloses each of the cells is pulled into the shape of a flat disc, spreading the pigment of the cell for maximum exposure of that colour. When the animal relaxes, the pigment is compressed into obscurity.

By rapid expansion and contraction of the appropriate muscles, these animals can send a rippling pattern of colours across their bodies that puts the colour changes effected by any other animal to shame.

Other colour changes occur over much longer periods – an example being the gradual loss of the spotted, camouflaging, coat of the fawn of North America's white-tailed deer.

As the fawn (which also emits very little telltale scent) matures from its springtime birth into its first winter, the spots give way to the brown and grey-brown coat of adulthood. The fawn makes full use of its spotted coat, which blends so perfectly with the sun-spotted floor of its forest home, by crouching low to the ground and even stretching its head and neck out along the ground whenever threatened. The adult deer retains the ability to remain quite motionless for long periods of danger and in addition it gains the ability of bounding speed for fast escape.

The white-tailed deer will never again wear its spotted coat, but other animals see such camouflaging changes come and go each year of their lives.

The snowshoe hare and the ptarmigan of the Arctic and subarctic regions, for example, moult from their summer brown or grey colouring to white each autumn, which gives them the camouflage they will need to survive in a snow-covered environment. And each spring, as the snows melt, they moult from their winter white into brown or grey for the same reason.

For the ptarmigan the change is much slower in the male than it is in the female, so that he becomes much more conspicuous than the female, as she sits, barely visible on a nest of new eggs. This variation may allow the male to assist in the tasks of bringing up the next generation by distracting predators with his continuing bright colours.

Similarly the radiantly yellow male American goldfinch makes seasonal changes between the colour for which it is named during the spring and summer mating season and the dull olive of the female during the relatively colourless seasons of late autumn and winter.

Although the colour change in most male birds is not quite so marked as that of the goldfinch, the majority do display their brightest colours during the mating season. Attraction of the female is the primary reason for this.

The male frigate bird of the tropical oceans carries the mating colouration act to an extreme. An enormous, bright red pouch on its breast – used solely to attract passing females to its relatively small nesting area – remains inflated only during the breeding season.

LEFT To move from its white winter plumage to its summertime brown, and later from its brown to white coat, the ptarmigan moults in spring and fall.

LEFT Some predators, like this long-tailed weasel, also undergo colour transformations to match the season.

Other species take a more active role in the use of colour to attract mates. The male bowerbirds of Australia and New Guinea, for example, build and decorate bowers to enhance the attraction of whatever plumage they already have. To illustrate this activity, let us consider the male satin bowerbird.

First, he clears an area of about .3 sq metres (3 square feet) of all debris. In that clearing he builds a pathway of 30 centimetres (1 foot) or more, lined with straight sticks which he pushes into the ground in two parallel rows.

At the south end of the pathway, he sets up his theatre with a carpet of grass and small twigs. He decorates this area with an array of blue, yellow and yellow-green objects such as feathers, berries and seashells. When humans are nearby, the decorations will also include glass beads, tinsel, coloured bits of wool, buttons and the like. This species' colour preference in its decorations seems to correspond to the plumage of the male and female.

Next, the bird paints the inside of this bower with blue juice from berries that it crushes in its beak for just this purpose. Some species make a black paint from charcoal dust and saliva and apply that with a bit of bark.

The bird remains constantly busy, removing older flowers and berries, replacing them with fresh ones and sprucing up with fresh coats of berry paint. When the time finally arrives for its courtship dance, the bird will hold up a bright blue object that it has saved for this purpose as it moves through the gyrations.

The golder bowerbird adds a variation to this theme by building a bower that is 3 metres (10 feet) tall and has a sapling as its centre. Lauterbach's bowerbird decorates with thousands of pebbles, bits of grass and sticks formed into four walls and lined with grass.

The brown bowerbird builds a cone of moss about the size of a man's fist, with a radiating pile of twigs about its sapling base. Other twigs are jammed into the mass to make it firm. The thatching eventually becomes so thick that the bower is waterproof. In front of this structure, the bird places a moss garden onto which it scatters brightly coloured flowers and fruits.

The mammals' most notable representative in this mating colouration is the male mandrill, a west African monkey with a bright red and blue face and blue genitals.

In such mating strategies, bright colouration is an attraction. But just as often it serves to repel or warn.

LEFT *The bright red pouch of the male frigate bird is inflated only during the mating season.*

ABOVE *The various species of bowerbird do not rely on their plumage alone to attract a mate and painstakingly construct elaborate bowers, often decorating them with any coloured objects they can gather such as feathers and berries, or even tinsel and glass beads.*

The skunk is the classic example of this warning colouration. The strong black and white pattern of its fur signals the animal's location on even the darkest night. At the same time, the skunk is ready to give any predator that fails to heed that warning a potent spray from its anal stink-glands. The skunk will often stamp its forefeet and flaunt its tail as further warning before letting loose with the spray.

Similarly, the shorthorn grasshoppers are brightly coloured and somewhat sluggish in comparison to more camouflaged grasshoppers. They also discharge a highly offensive foam when threatened. The colour serves as a warning of the foam. Some species even congregate in masses to enhance their conspicuousness, while others extend brightly coloured hindwings for the same purpose.

The various species of South American arrow-poison frogs, are all conspicuously coloured in yellows, blues and reds. Few predators risk this amphibian's potent poison, which acts on the central nervous system. The fire salamander of Europe offers a similar black and yellow warning of its milky skin secretion which is potent enough to kill any small predator.

Some quite poisonous animals, however, have not developed the bright colouration to warn of their potency. The *Bufo marinus,* a toad with a poison that has killed large dogs, has retained its cryptic colouring as part of its ambush of prey. When threatened, it warns of its poison by inflating itself and issuing warning cries.

Still other species have evolved the bright colouration of similar toxic species without developing the poison. They thus take advantage of the warning scheme without having any real clout of their own to back it up.

RIGHT A male peacock fans its colourful tail feathers to attract the mating attention of the much plainer female.

RIGHT Day or night, a would-be attacker can read the black-and-white warning of the skunk.

BELOW The colouring of the harmless milk snake helps it to avoid encounters with many predators that stay clear of what they think to be the highly venomous coral snake.

Several quite palatable (at least to their natural predators) species of butterfly closely resemble the markings of the monarch butterfly, and thus take advantage of the toxic nature of the monarch. However, only the monarch stores the heart-poisons, similar to digitalis, from the milkweed plants which form its entire diet. Similarly, the North American milk snake is also a naturally coloured mimic of the poisonous coral snake. However, some animals are much more proactive in their mimicry. The harmless crested rat of Africa, for example, when threatened, parts its outer fur to display black and white stripes similar to those of the aggressive and smelly zorille, a skunk-like animal also native to Africa.

Bright colouration can also allow for trickery. Predators of species such as the Malaysian back-to-front butterfly or the marine butterfly fish often mistakenly attack the deceptively coloured rear end of their intended victim, allowing the butterfly or fish to dart off in its true frontal direction.

But colouration serves the purpose of concealment at least as often as warning or trickery, whether the animal purposefully creates that concealment or not.

For example, the masking crab of the world's oceans builds its disguise by attaching pieces of seaweed to the hooked bristles on its carapace and legs.

Many more species capture their protective colouring through their diet. Sea slugs gain their pigments from the sponges on which they feed and rest, even incorporating the digested sponges' needle-like spicules into their own skin. Caterpillars of the pug moth match the colours of the flowers on which they are feeding, be they pink thistles or blue scabious.

The stick-caterpillar of the peppered moth also blends well with the colouring and texture of whatever food source it lives on, from birch to oak to lichen-covered wood. It is thought that this adaptation is triggered by some genetic mechanism when the caterpillar first hatches from its egg and perceives its surroundings.

Although the frogmouths, several species of medium-sized birds in southeast Asia and Central America, do

EXTRAORDINARY ANIMALS

BELOW *When seen from distance, the stark black-and-white pattern of the zebra actually lends a countershading effect to the animal.*

RIGHT *Sea slugs absorb and use the poison from the sponges that they prey upon.*

86

RIGHT The gradual tonal changes in the African lion's fur allow it to lie in wait at water holes, relatively invisible to its prey.

not develop their camouflage markings through their diet, they nonetheless make the most of the concealment. When threatened they hold their head, neck and body stiff and upright, with their eyes closed to narrow slits, further nudging their tree-bark colouring to achieve the look of a broken stump or limb. The female lays her single egg atop a branch and incubates it by sitting with her body oriented along the branch rather than across.

The frogmouth's cousin, the European nightjar, is cryptically coloured for forest floor rather than tree limbs, but the bird performs similar manoeuvres to enhance the camouflage effect. The nightjar closes its eyes to narrow slits, and changes its body position in relation to the sun so as to cast the minimum shadow possible. On the nest, it relies on its cryptic colouring to conceal the eggs it is sitting on, and will flush only as a last option.

Some animals' colouration may not appear at all concealing at first glance. The vivid black and white stripes of a zebra, for instance, are very conspicuous when viewed close up. However, when seen from a distance, the pattern – which actually has dark stripes that become wider on the animal's back – blends to afford the animal a countershading effect.

Similarly the gradual tonal changes in the relatively monochromatic colouring of some animals, such as the African lion, offers much more camouflage under certain conditions than might at first be assumed. The lion can lie at a water hole in quite adequate concealment to await the coming of a prey animal.

A few animals gain their camouflage through the lack of colour. The transparent wings of the glass-winged butterfly, for example, allow the colour of the foliage beneath them to show through.

Still others combine colouration with body shape to achieve their concealment. Trying to distinguish the South American leaf fish from a leaf, the Malaysian praying mantis from its twiggy environment or several species of African spider from the acacia thorns that envelope them can become exercises in futility.

The Builders

Man is the undisputed master builder of the world. Of course, nearly all of what we build is artificial, often destroying natural places to make way for itself. And given only the raw materials, most of us could construct less than adequate shelter for ourselves.

In the wild there are other animals that amaze and intrigue us with their innate, yet superior, building abilities. Admittedly, much of what they do arises from reflex and would continue even without the originally intended function, but their constructions have that unmistakable quality of something learned from experience.

North America's beaver is generally the first creature named in a discussion of natural builders. Because the constructions of this large rodent deserve such attention, we shall not break that tradition here.

The beaver is well adapted for aquatic life, with webbed hind feet; a large, flat tail that functions as a rudder; valves that close off the ears and nostrils when submerged; clear membranes to protect the eyes; flaps of skin to seal the mouth; a gland-produced waterproofing for its fur; a thick layer of fat for insulation against the cold of the water; and lungs that can carry a 15-

RIGHT *A beaver chews on a freshly cut aspen branch.*

BELOW *The beaver of North America is the undisputed champion builder of the animal world.*

LEFT *With mud, sticks, logs and rocks, the beaver creates its own pond by damming a mountain stream and fashions its own secure home, the lodge.*

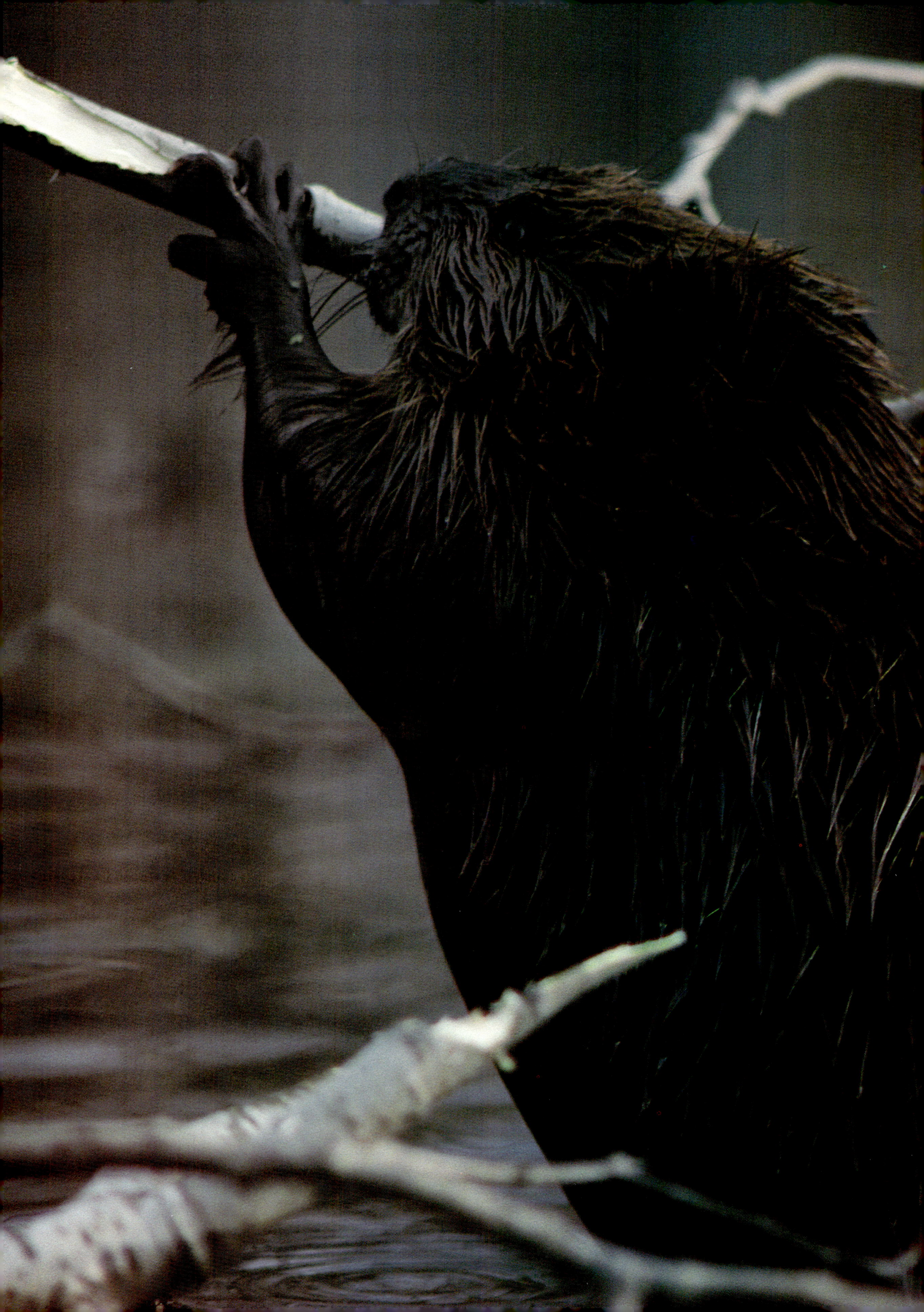

CUT-AWAY VIEW OF A BEAVER LODGE

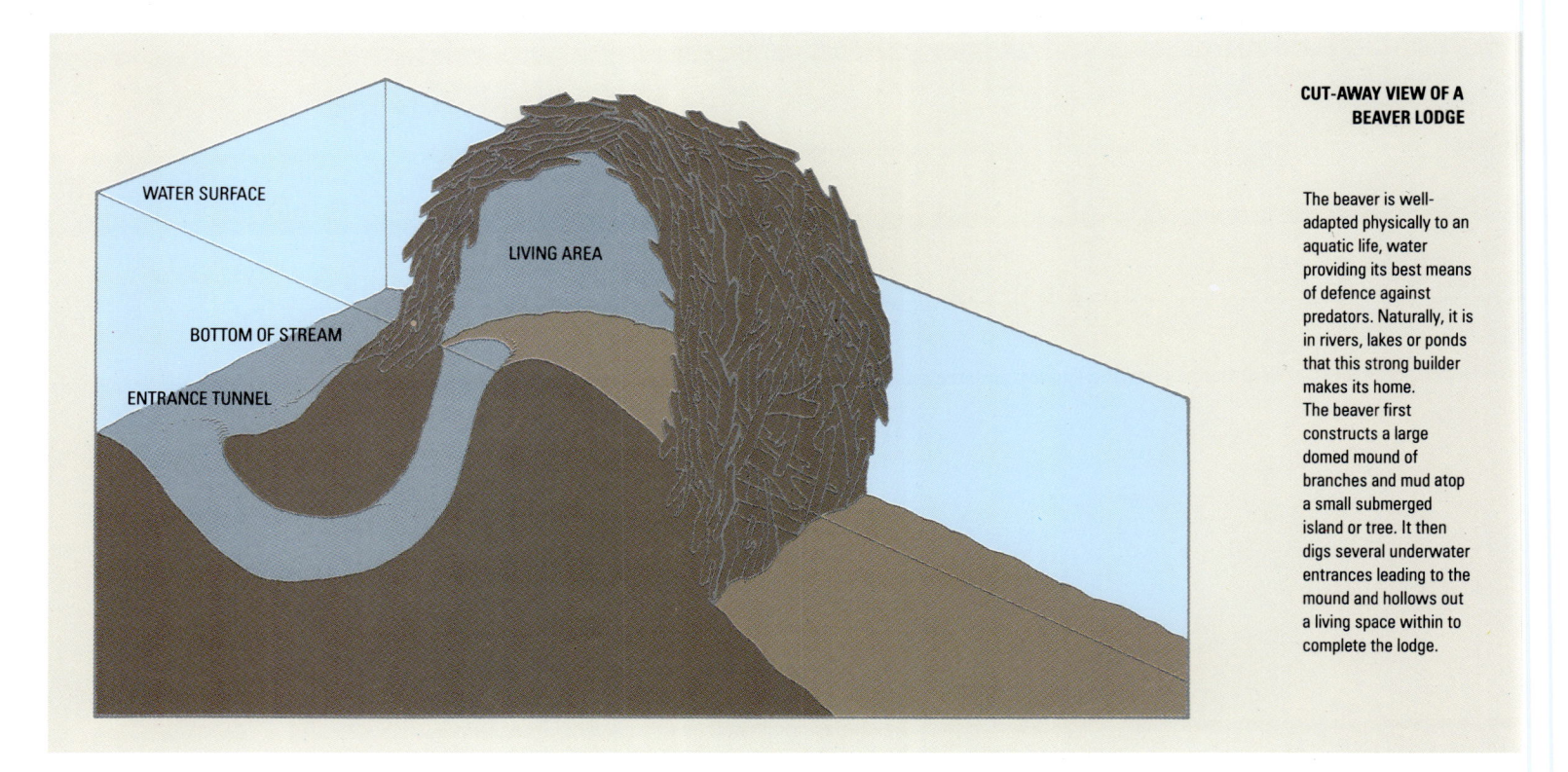

The beaver is well-adapted physically to an aquatic life, water providing its best means of defence against predators. Naturally, it is in rivers, lakes or ponds that this strong builder makes its home. The beaver first constructs a large domed mound of branches and mud atop a small submerged island or tree. It then digs several underwater entrances leading to the mound and hollows out a living space within to complete the lodge.

BELOW RIGHT A domelike mound of branches and mud forms the beavers lodge.

minute supply of air. The watery depths are always the beaver's first and best defence against any threat. Is it any wonder that the animal seeks those depths wherever it goes?

Generally, beavers living along large rivers and lakes will be content with the existing aquatic environment, digging simple underwater entrances to a hollow living space in the bank or shore. They might construct crude lodges atop this hollow, or they might construct lodges in the shallows of a lake.

However those members of the family Castoridae that make their homes in smaller rivers and lakes, streams and ponds build the dams and lodges for which the beaver is famous.

The dam is the first consideration when beavers move into a new area, which must have an ample and accessible food supply. Tree branches are the primary building materials for the dam. The beaver cuts the tree upstream by gnawing around its base, and can 'fell' a softwood of 13-centimetre (5-inch) diameter in about three minutes. 'Teams' may jointly cut large trees. Using its superior sense of hearing, the beaver can usually tell by the crackling of the wood when the trunk is about to break, although the animal occasionally does not get away from the falling tree before it is too late.

The wood is then floated and carried in the beaver's teeth to the dam site, where it is weighted down with mud, gravel and even large stones. As the dam grows, mud is added to the downstream side and to the crest as a reinforcement.

Dam designs vary widely. In waterways with relatively swift currents, the dam might be bowed upstream to lessen the force of the water pressure.

The lodge is a domelike mound of branches and mud, at least 1.8 metres (6 feet) tall and as much as 15 metres (50 feet) in diameter, with several underwater entrances below the freezing level. It will generally be built well away from the shores of the pond, but around something solid such as a small island or a submerged tree. To create the hollow living space inside, the beaver tunnels into the mound it has built, gnawing off all unnecessary branches. Part of the lodge roof is left unsecured to permit adequate ventilation. Some large ponds have more than one lodge.

Stockpiles of woody food – aspen, poplar, willow, maple and birch are preferred – are built up inside the lodge, as well as being stored throughout the pond.

Although the beaver is not as constantly busy as popular belief would have it, repair is a common part of its daily life. As the water area behind the dam grows, the beaver increases both the width and depth of the dam to accommodate it. During periods of flood, however, spillways may be created to alleviate pressure.

The beaver also builds mounds, which are small piles of sticks and mud where the animal deposits scent from anal glands to mark family territory. Canals are often dug to transport logs to the dam site, as safer travel routes and to divert excess waterflow from the dam.

The colony that normally occupies a beaver dam consists of the two parents, probably mated for life, the current year's litter of kits and last year's litter. Young ones are generally driven off by the parents at two years, unless they first leave on their own.

Many generations may continue work on the dam, and some of these constructions are believed to be more than 1,000 years old.

Although the beaver builds to fulfil its own environmental needs, the alterations that it brings to the landscape benefit many other creatures. Immediately the presence of the pond offers a new and expanded habitat, while soil carried downstream and trapped by the dam eventually will give rise to a rich meadow.

Humans too can often benefit from the beaver's work, but there are times when the site chosen by the animal comes into conflict with the purposes of man. This can lead to a tug-of-war, as man works to dig out or dynamite the dam, while the beaver seems to be able to rebuild almost overnight. In some areas where beavers are active as much as $2,000 (about £1,280) per year is spent on each culvert or bridge to keep it clear.

ABOVE Towing a branch, a beaver swims to its underwater storage pile of food for the winter.

EXTRAORDINARY ANIMALS

LEFT A single honeybee egg is contained in each one of these six-sided cells. Note that all the cells are not exactly the same shape and size, contrary to popular myth.

ABOVE Honeybee larvae are seen in various stages of development in these cells in the hive.

LEFT A colony of honeybees works in its hive.

Many methods have been tried to outwit these rodent engineers, usually ending with the beavers figuring out how to maintain their dam despite all these methods. At such times, removal of the animals has generally been the solution.

However the Maine Department of Inland Fisheries and Wildlife recently experimented with a new method that appeared to solve the problem. A framework of metal fence posts is built, on which an array of five or six 10 centimetre (4 inch) perforated pipes is laid. The downstream ends of the pipes are anchored low in the beaver dam, while the upstream ends of the 6-metre (20-foot)-long pipes are held at the desired level over deep water. The pipes are laid side by side, several feet apart, and a protective cage is fashioned over the ends to keep away floating debris.

No matter how high the beavers build the dam, the siphon pipes continue flowing water through the structure, maintaining optimum water levels for wildlife while protecting roads and timberlands from flooding.

The honeybee is another animal builder generally associated with the word 'busy'.

The life of the hive, although focused on the queen and the new brood, is really maintained by the workers. Most of the 20,000 to 50,000 bees in a hive are workers, with specialized glands for everything from making honey into wax to producing milk to feed the queen and brood.

At the center of the hive, the brood is kept in one compact area. Pollen is stored next to the brood for the nurse bees to use in producing their bee milk. In the

ABOVE Some African termite mounds have been measured at more than six metres (20 feet) in height. This mound was found in Kruger National Park, South Africa.

next outer layer, the honey is stored in combs. Vacant gaps anywhere in the hive are filled with resin collected from trees, which serves to control the growth of mould.

To build a new comb, the cells of which are constructed vertically, the bees place a string of wax along the ceiling to serve as their guide. On both sides of this, they form a layer of cylinders, which eventually become hexagonal because of the natural pressure inherent in the comb design. The cells are not all of an identical shape and dimension, as commonly believed.

Although every house bee is capable of building an entire cell on its own, this never occurs. Every cell is the result of a team effort. The current work of any one house bee is always determined by the needs of the entire colony, rather than by that of one bee.

The house bees also provide air conditioning as needed in the hive, by fanning their wings to divert air currents. Temperature at the all-important brood nest cannot be allowed to vary more than a couple of degrees from 32° C (90° F) and humidity must be maintained at 35 to 40 percent.

Ants and termites, which are actually more closely related to cockroaches than to ants, follow similar caste systems within their nests. In their simplest forms, these nests are simply excavations in the earth or rotting wood.

In the northern hemisphere ants add a mound of earth, leaf bits, sticks and debris above the underground nest for extra insulation. The mound might be more than 90 centimetres (3 feet) tall and represent several months of labour by millions of ants. Its surface remains in an almost constant state of change, as the ants make adjustments for temperature control. This activity can include the digging of ventilation holes, 'fluffing' of existing material and the addition of new material. The shape of the mound also affects the temperature, and its longest slope usually faces south to take in the most sunshine possible.

Much more elaborate mounds are built by the compass termites of Australia. These mounds, which can reach heights of more than 3.7 metres (12 feet), are always constructed on a north-south axis with the narrowest edge facing the heat of midday and the broader edges receiving the less intense sun earlier and later.

The macrotermes, an African termite species, build the largest nests. Their mounds, which might be 6 metres (20 feet) tall and more than 27 metres (90 feet) in diameter, begin as an underground chamber, where they develop a fungus garden around the royal cell. A dome is built above the garden as the nest grows, and new gardens and domes are added around the original, constantly swelling the overall structure.

Spiders are also among the master builders of the natural world. Many construct one of four types of web: an irregular maze of silken threads, a closely woven sheet, a sheet with a net above it, and a series of radiating lines of thread.

THE BUILDERS

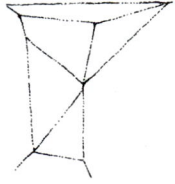

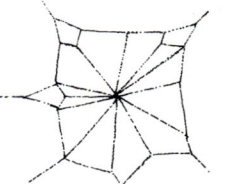

BELOW The web created by the orb-web spider is an intricate maze of radiating lines constructed within an anchored framework.

LEFT An orb-weaving spider of the Aranidae family clings to its dew-coated web in the early morning.

EXTRAORDINARY ANIMALS

ABOVE Close-up view of the nest of an African weaverbird. Each grass piece was thrust into place to create the thatched basket.

RIGHT A golden weaver with its own version of a woven nest, along the coast of Kenya.

96

To begin a web, an orb-web spider secretes a protein-rich silky substance from its spinnerets, which forms a small fan-shaped kite. As the spider secretes more silk, the kite is carried off by the breeze. If it settles on a twig or some other stationary object, it will adhere to that object. If there is no contact, the spider retrieves the line, eats it and tries again.

After contact has been achieved, the spider attaches the end of the line it still holds and begins crossing. As the spider moves, it secretes a new line and winds in the first line. At the midway point, it attaches the two lines and drops to the ground, secreting a third anchor line as it falls.

On the ground, the spider sidesteps a few paces to give the web a slant and attaches the third anchor. Within this frame, it now builds a series of radiating or irregular lines and sticky lines that will ensnare its prey.

The whole process would seem to be completely automatic and guided only by instinct, but the spider does gauge the results (by touch, not sight) as the work progresses and will make changes. Some young spiders will reconstruct and reposition several times before being satisfied with their results.

The largest webs are built by the tropical orb weavers. These can have diameters of as much as 1.5 metres (5 feet) and supporting guide-lines as long as 6 metres (20 feet). Other species, construct quite different structures to capture their prey.

The purse-web spider, for example, builds a silk-lined tunnel that extends upwards about 45 centimetres (18 inches) along the base of a tree. The spider camouflages its tunnel with vegetation collected nearby. When something walks on the tunnel, the whole structure vibrates. The spider bites through the web and pulls the hapless insect inside, repairing the damage later.

The trapdoor spider uses its powerful jaws to dig a vertical shaft, just wide enough to turn around inside, down into the earth. It seals the top of the shaft with a hinged lid, camouflaged with vegetation, and coats the tunnel with a waterproof lining of saliva-soaked earth and a sheet of silk.

The shaft is used in courtship, mating and rearing the young, but the spider also ambushes its prey through the trapdoor. When an insect passes by the door, the

ABOVE A colony of weaverbird nests hang from a tree in Amboseli, Kenya.

RIGHT *A pair of ravens taunt an osprey as it nests on the shore of Yellowstone Lake in Yellowstone National Park.*

FAR RIGHT *The entrance to the nest of a weaver finch.*

spider lunges outside and grabs it, all the while propping open the door with its hind legs for a quick escape route.

Living in an aquatic environment, the water spider can trap air bubbles in the thick hair that covers its body and use that trapped air to breathe underwater. But the supply of air that can be held in this way is not sufficient for extended submerged activity, so the spider constructs an oxygen reservoir.

First it weaves a horizontal web among plant stems. From the surface it ferries small bubbles of air which are then released under the web. As the amount of air held by the web grows, the web is pushed into a dome-shaped tent.

The spider waits inside this supply of air to grab passing prey, such as water fleas and gnat larvae. It also mates in the female's bubble, sealing the eggs into the roof with a sheet of silk.

Solitary potter and mason wasps create a reservoir of a different nature, a living reservoir to supply food for their young. They build small, cell-like receptacles of saliva-moistened clay along the stem of a plant. They drop a poison-paralyzed caterpillar into each receptacle, lay their eggs on top of it and then seal the receptacle. When the eggs hatch, the young have a ready supply of food.

No discussion of animal builders would be complete without a look at bird nests, of which there is an almost unlimited variety, from the thimble-sized version of the bee hummingbird to the massive stack of sticks and twigs of the bald eagle.

One of the largest nests ever recorded was built in Ohio over a period of 35 years by several generations of bald eagles. It measured nearly 3 metres (9 feet) in width and 3.7 metres (12 feet) in depth, and when a severe storm brought it to the ground the remains weighed 2 tons.

The stick-mud-grass configuration may be the most instantly recognized nest, but many birds create quite different structures.

Some, like the pileated woodpecker, carve their nest into the stump of a rotting tree. Others, such as the West African bee-eaters, tunnel deep into a stream bank. Still others, like the cave swifts of Malaya, attach strings of mucus-like saliva which hardens on contact with air to cave walls.

The rufous-breasted castlebuilder's nest might look like simply a mass of twigs from the outside. But inside, it is actually a turret-like entrance of fine twigs, a hallway carpeted with shed reptile skin and a nest chamber lined with a mat of green leaves.

The many species of weaverbird in Africa and Asia construct thatched baskets by thrusting (never pulling) fresh, flexible vegetation together. Some species form communal nests of more than 100 individual baskets.

Africa's tailor bird sews two broad leaves together with plant fibres, using its beak as the needle, to construct its nest.

A female short-billed marsh wren returns to her dome-shaped nest with fresh food for her nestlings.

BELOW With crayfish in tow, a barred owl returns to its nestlings in the hollow of a tree.

ABOVE The first experience with birds' nests for many Americans is the quite common mud-nest of the American robin.

Commonly one or both of the birds of most species will sit atop the pair's eggs in whatever nest they've built, incubating the next generation. But there are exceptions.

The male emperor and king penguins of icy Antarctica hold the single egg on top of their feet and snuggled into the warmth of their lower body during the two months of incubation. The mallee fowl of Asia brings added warmth to its nest by laying its eggs atop decaying vegetable matter and covering them with loose, sandy soil. As the vegetation decays it gives off heat, which the bird regulates to a near constant temperature by changing the amount of soil atop the nest.

Nest-building is by no means limited to the avian fraternity. Eggs of the African grey tree frog are deposited into a nest made of mucus exuded by the female and whipped into a froth by the back legs of the male. This glob is left hanging in trees over water, allowing the tadpoles to drop into their next-stage home after initial development.

The male stickleback fish uses a secretion from his kidneys to hold his nest of wood and plant bits together and attached to weed branches. When he has finished constructing the mass, he bores a tunnel hole through it and enlarges the interior by pushing up on the ceiling from inside. He will work to entice as many females as possible to enter the nest for spawning. If the nest be-

LEFT A prairie dog town might have 50 burrows, each one holding as many as 15 of the small ground squirrels.

comes damaged, he will make repairs immediately.

The fry hatch about one week later, but remain close to the nest in a tight mass protected by the male. Any that wander too far from the sanctuary will be sucked into the male's mouth and returned to the group. After a few weeks of this, the male loses his protective instinct and the now-ready young are allowed to disperse.

On land, the harvest mouse of European and Asian grain fields, meadows and marshes, forms a similar nest of vegetation. The mouse first interlaces leaves of standing weed stalks to form a base for the nest. It then pulls blades of grass and leaves through its teeth to cut them to thin shreds which are woven into the sides and dome-roof of the nest.

The finished nest is a firm, dense ball with one entrance hole. The inside is padded with seed down and shredded leaves to finish the process, which requires five to ten hours. A similar nest is constructed for each of the several litters of three to five young that the mouse produces each year.

The nest of the dormouse is quite similar, although much more accomplished, consisting of a sphere of long summer grasses suspended between plant stems. It has been described as the most sophisticated structure built by any mammal.

Although no one has ever described the burrows, or setts, of the European badger in that way, they are none-theless impressive for their sheer size. Some have been measured as extending more than 90 metres (300 feet) in length, with as many as 50 entrances and three storeys. Such large labyrinths of passageways are usually the work of several badger families. Other animals, such as foxes for instance, make regular uses of the lesser tunnels of the sett.

The badger doesn't hibernate, but it does sleep away much of the winter in a deep chamber lined with dry vegetation. The animal occasionally carries this 'mattress' outside to air it out for a few hours before returning it to the sleeping chamber.

Although North America has its own species of badger, the tunnel-building champion on this side of the Atlantic is the prairie dog. A 'town' might have 40 to 50 burrows, each one housing as many as 15 individuals in separate branches off the main burrow. Each family group will defend its burrow from those of its neighbours. At least one of these small ground squirrels will stand guard over the 'town' at all times. A single cry from this sentinel will send all the prairie dogs diving for safety.

In the 19th century there were probably millions of prairie dogs in the American West. Their 'towns' were reported to cover several square miles each. The animal still lives in the West, although man has reduced its numbers greatly.

A Varied Menu

Diet among the animals is as varied as animals themselves. For nearly every plant and animal on earth there is some other animal that eats it.

Some animals apparently have quite catholic tastes, consuming whatever comes their way. The opossum of North America will eat anything digestible, at one moment it may be a scavenger, dining on a road-kill; later it may turn predator to snatch up a smaller animal; still later, as a herbivore, it will munch on some new plant growth.

Other animals have extremely discriminating palates. For example, a relative of the opossum, the koala of Australia and Tasmania (which, though a marsupial, is the original 'teddy bear') eats only eucalyptus leaves, and only from trees that are producing a specific oil at the time.

RIGHT *One of the most restricted diets among all animals is that of the koala. The furry native of Australia and Tasmania eats only the leaves of eucalyptus trees that are producing a specific oil.*

RIGHT *The diet of the opossum is one of the most diverse on the face of the earth, including nearly all the vegetable and animal matter with which the marsupial comes into contact.*

Other animals display less specialized diets, which are nonetheless extraordinarily simply because of the huge quantity of the food consumed. For example, the largest of all animals, the blue whale, feeds on comparatively tiny krill, which are shrimp-sized crustaceans, but a large whale might need a full ton of the small creatures to fill its gut. The apparently odd choice of food for such a massive beast makes more sense when one considers the fact that only such tiny organisms are able to reproduce fast enough and in quantities sufficient to keep the whale fed.

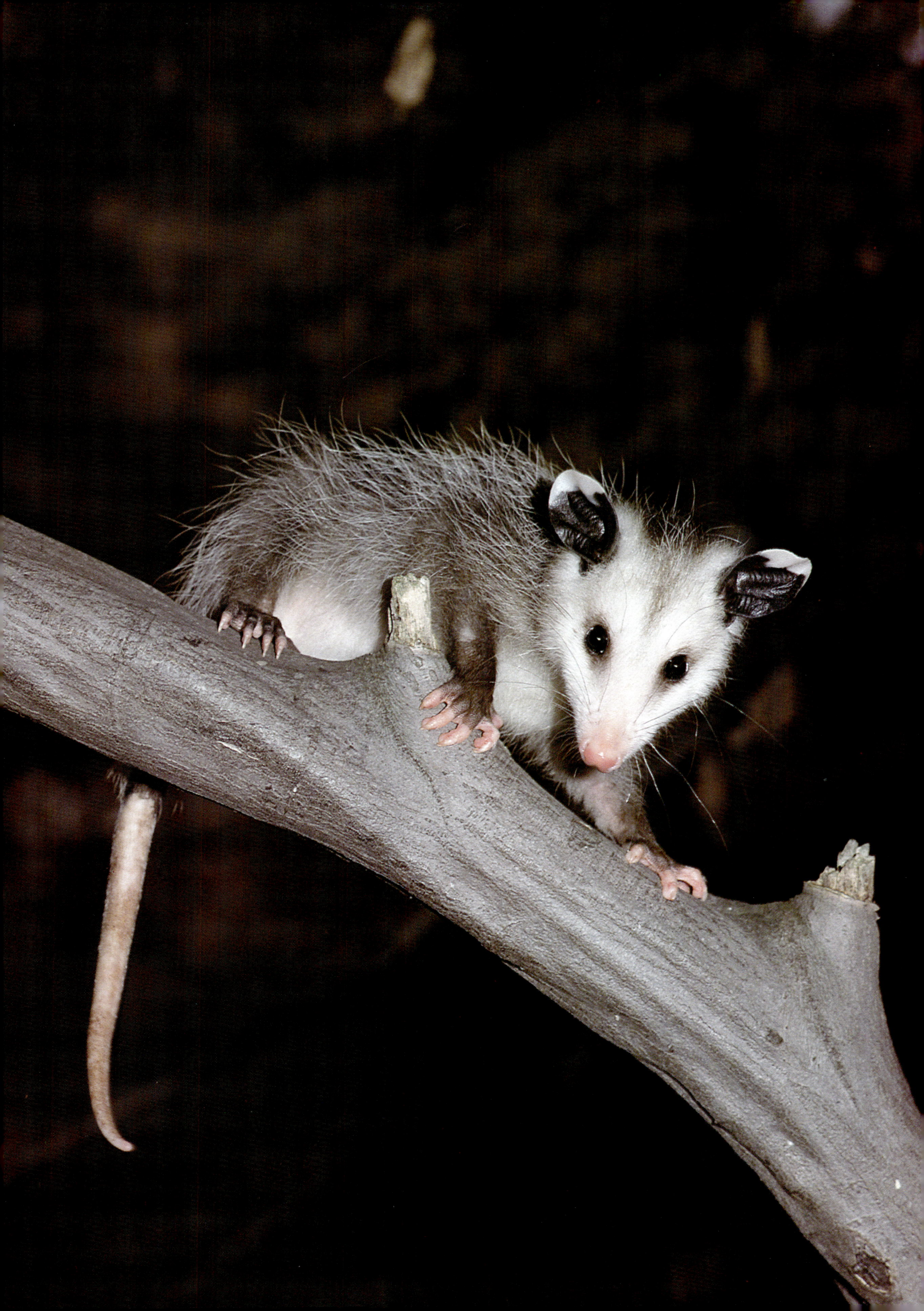

LEFT An African elephant spends all but four to six hours of every day foraging for its vegetarian diet.

Another large creature, the African elephant spends from 18 to 20 hours of every day dining on grass, roots, bark, wood, fruit and bamboo. Nearly half of that food passes through the animal undigested. This inefficient use of food is accompanied by plenty of stomach rumblings. Over that same period, the elephant will drink as much as 95 litres (84 British quarts) of water.

The camel is legendary for its ability to spend extended periods in arid regions with minimal water. Although most tales of this ability exaggerate the time frame involved, there is some truth behind them. In one test a camel was kept from water for eight days. It lost nearly a quarter of its body weight through dehydration and took on a pathetically emaciated appearance, but it survived. A human being would have died of heatstroke after losing half that much. When it was offered water the camel drank bucket after bucket, regaining its former appearance and good health. In other experiments 'dry' camels have been known to drink as much as 143 litres (126 British quarts) in 10 minutes.

Several abilities combine to allow a camel to withstand such extremes of water loss. It loses water from its blood more slowly, has a high tolerance for low water content in its body and evaporates its internal water much less because its body permits relatively large internal temperature variations of as much as the temperature difference between night and day.

The hippopotamus, which is one of the more gluttonous animals on earth, makes a strange use of the food that passes through its body. Dominant males use their short tails to spatter their excrement as territorial markings, in contests with opposing males and to impress females. The one that sprays the most wins.

Like hippos, bears take in large volumes of food, when they aren't hibernating. Although the question of whether bears go into true hibernation continues to be debated, they have demonstrated the ability to stay in their dens from two-and-a-half to seven months without taking any food or water. They also go without urinating or defecating during that same time.

A VARIED MENU

ABOVE *Camels can go several days without water and then quickly replace their lost body weight at the first available source.*

LEFT *The camel's body permits relatively large internal temperature variations, which is one of the mechanisms that allow the animal to survive periods without water.*

RIGHT *Bears have been known to stay in their dens from two-and-a-half to seven months without taking food or water, and without urinating or defecating.*

LEFT The hippopotamus is one of the most gluttonous animals on earth.

The groundhog, or woodchuck, has also demonstrated the ability to stay underground during extended periods of winter weather.

During hibernation, the bear's blood carries a nearly constant level of water, with small losses being replaced by the breakdown of body fat reserves. Waste materials are recycled.

Some animal species have developed mutually beneficial, symbiotic relationships based partly on the food habits of one, or the other, or both. Ants 'herd' aphids much as man herds cattle to produce some of their food supply. The ants actually 'milk' the plant-destroying aphids for a sweet, yellow liquid which is a by-product of the aphids' digestion of plant starches. In return, the ants provide protection for the aphids and, sometimes, their eggs. Some species of ant even build tiny bark shelters to shield their 'cows', and if a shelter is destroyed will move the aphid to another.

Several species of hermit crab and sea anemone have developed this relationship so thoroughly that they cannot survive without one another. The poisonous anemone provides defence and, in turn, shares in the crab's food. A species of crab in the Indian Ocean carries its stinging sea anemone in its claws, poking it at unwanted intruders.

Other animals have developed specialized body parts to combat the constant food problem. Many deep-sea fish have gaping mouths and extendable stomachs so as not to pass up any potential meal, no matter how large, in their under-populated environment.

Snakes are able to perform similar feats, with their long, flexible jaws. The snake's grasping teeth point into its body, holding the prey securely but sliding out of and into the food as the snake pulls itself over it. The prey animal is thus swallowed whole.

Water fleas, common in any pond water, have developed another part of their body, their five pairs of legs, as a specialized feeding mechanism. Not needed for movement, which the animal achieves with its antennae, the legs instead set up a constant flow of water through the flea. Bristles on some of the legs snag whatever edible organisms are caught in the current and pass them to the mouth.

However, only one animal other than man has actually developed a tool to help it obtain food. The chimpanzee fashions twigs into instruments with which it pulls termites from their holes.

ABOVE The snake consumes its prey whole, enabled by flexible jaws and inward-pointing, grasping teeth that move in and out of the food as the snake pulls itself over its prey.

EXTRAORDINARY ANIMALS

The Numbers Game

Humans do not rate highly in many comparisons of natural attributes to those creatures that still make daily use of their physiques and abilities in a constant struggle to survive. But in two numerical categories man does have the advantage: lifespan and total population.

Very few animals live longer than man's average 70 years, and only a few others come close. Sponges seem to have no known upper limits to their lives; they are theoretically immortal. Colonies of sea anemone have been kept in captivity for nearly 100 years and still showed no indication of being any closer to their demise than when they were first collected. The European freshwater clam can be as old as 115 years, and the lumbering Galapagos tortoise passes the century mark. The sturgeon lives at least 75 years, probably many more, while the graceful swan can reach 70.

Among mammals, those that approach humans' longevity are the Asian elephant, 65; the sperm whale, which lives more than 50 years, sometimes more than 70; and the gorilla, which has reached the age of 50 in captivity. Some non-mammals with similarly long lifespans include the American eel, 70 in captivity; Andean condor, more than 60 in captivity; giant salamander, 55; alligator, more than 50; and lobster, 50.

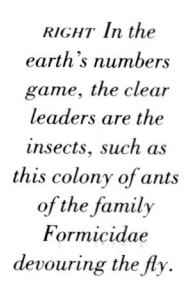

RIGHT *In the earth's numbers game, the clear leaders are the insects, such as this colony of ants of the family Formicidae devouring the fly.*

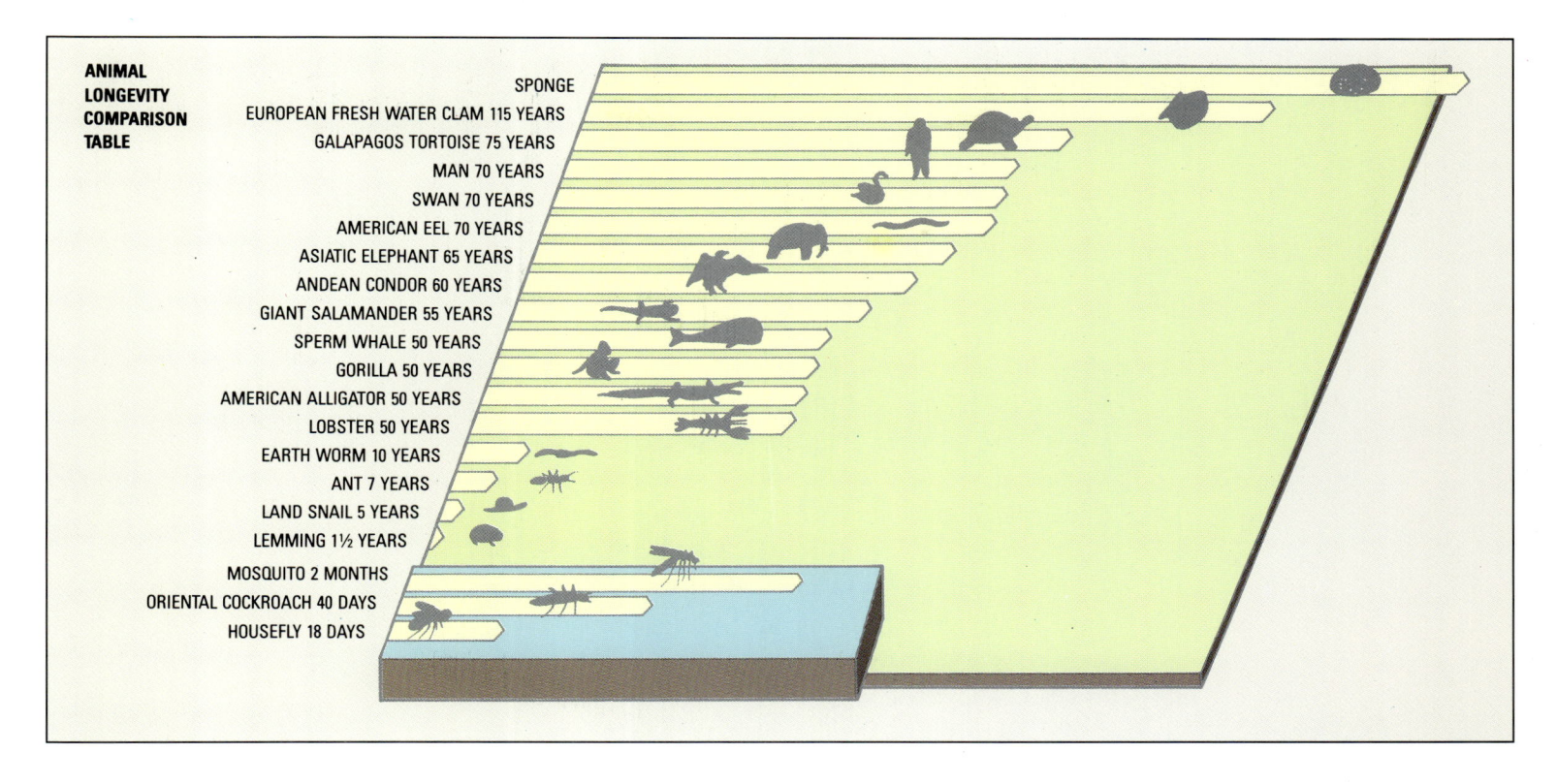

ANIMAL LONGEVITY COMPARISON TABLE

- SPONGE
- EUROPEAN FRESH WATER CLAM 115 YEARS
- GALAPAGOS TORTOISE 75 YEARS
- MAN 70 YEARS
- SWAN 70 YEARS
- AMERICAN EEL 70 YEARS
- ASIATIC ELEPHANT 65 YEARS
- ANDEAN CONDOR 60 YEARS
- GIANT SALAMANDER 55 YEARS
- SPERM WHALE 50 YEARS
- GORILLA 50 YEARS
- AMERICAN ALLIGATOR 50 YEARS
- LOBSTER 50 YEARS
- EARTH WORM 10 YEARS
- ANT 7 YEARS
- LAND SNAIL 5 YEARS
- LEMMING 1½ YEARS
- MOSQUITO 2 MONTHS
- ORIENTAL COCKROACH 40 DAYS
- HOUSEFLY 18 DAYS

Some shorter average lifespans belong to the ant, up to 15 years for the queen and up to 7 for a worker; land snail, up to 5; earthworm, 5 to 10; lemming, 1, possibly 1½; mosquito, 2 months; Oriental cockroach, 40 days; male housefly, 18 days.

In terms of overall population, man is the most abundant large animal. He is also on the increase, which is a primary reason that so many other animals – large and small – are declining.

The largest herds of mammals ever recorded were those during migrations of the springbok across the African plains. Reports from the mid-19th century tell of herds taking three days to pass. The last great migrations, near the end of the 19th century, included herds covering nearly 225 kilometres (140 miles) in length and 24 kilometres (15 miles) in width.

The New World's equivalent of this migrating animal was the bison of North America. Before Europeans set foot on the continent, an estimated 60 million of these huge beasts roamed free from coast to coast. Even after the wholesale slaughter had begun, during the settling of the American West, wagon trains reported having to wait for days until herds of bison passed. It is fair to add, however, that some experts on the bison have debated the accuracy of these reports.

At one time government policy actually advocated the extermination of the bison as a means to subdue the Indians, who relied heavily on the animal for everything from meat to clothing and shelter to fuel.

By the time a conservation ethic was beginning to develop at the beginning of the 20th century, fewer than 1,000 bison were left. However the struggle to keep the magnificent beast from extinction has been successful, and today there are more than 30,000 bison in United States and Canadian parks and private reserves.

The most abundant bird in the world is the red-bellied quelea, which inhabits the dry areas of Africa south of the Sahara. Existing in the thousands of millions, it poses a serious threat to grain crops. Breeding colonies can include more than 10 million birds each, and the annual purposeful killing of about a billion seems to have no lasting effect on the population.

North America's now extinct passenger pigeon may have come the closest of any other species to the quelea's numbers, with a total population estimated at 9 billion at one time. That, however, was before wholesale commercial slaughter started filling whole wagons with the birds to satisfy the demand for popular dishes of the 1800s such as pigeon pie.

The last passenger pigeon died on 1 September, 1914, in the Cincinnati Zoological Gardens. Its preserved body is held at the Smithsonian Institution.

All of these numbers seem minuscule when compared to the world's insect population, which has been estimated to be at least three to five times the population of all non-insect animals combined. A single square mile (that is, about 2.6 square kilometres) might contain more insects than the world contains humans. More than a million different species have been catalogued, again, more than all other species combined.

Of the insects the 1,500 species of springtail, which are found all over the globe, are the most abundant. More than 50,000 of these tiny insects might be found in one square metre (nearly 11 square feet) of soil. They earn their name with a springlike mechanism on the underside of their abdomen which can propel the insect several times its own length when released. The snow flea is the strangest of the group; it makes its home on the surface of snow, even in the Arctic and on glaciers.

ABOVE *Few animals outlive man or even come close to his average three score and ten years. A notable exception is the sponge which appears to live forever. This chart illustrates both those creatures with a notable longevity, comparable to man's, and those with a markedly short lifespan.*

The Movers

The migration of birds is a familiar aspect of the changing seasons. People who live in North America are accustomed to the sight of Canada geese flying south in the autumn and north in the spring. And one of the most delightful signs of spring is the return of songbirds to the garden.

These species, and a few others, have come to represent migration in the popular imagination; however some other animals are the true masters of the technique. For example, the arctic tern, flying from its breeding grounds in the northern latitudes to winter in the south, makes a yearly round trip of about 40,000 kilometres (25,000 miles). It may fly nearly non-stop for eight months of the year to accomplish its trans-global trip, which twice yearly takes it from one pole to the other.

Some baleen whales migrate 19,000 kilometres (12,000 miles) from polar to tropical regions for favourable feeding and calving conditions. The sub-polar waters of the north contain as much as 100 times the concentration of krill, the huge beasts' principal food, as the tropical waters. But those warmer waters to the south are more favourable for calving, requiring less energy of the young whales to maintain body temperature and thus allowing them to put more energy into growth and storing blubber for the winter.

Humpback whales, of which there are half-a-dozen populations in the Antarctic and three each in the north Atlantic and Pacific oceans, make this migration in small herds travelling about 355 kilometres (220 miles) per month. The blue whale makes the trip solo or in pairs.

Among the smallest migrants, the rufous hummingbird makes one of the longest round trips. This bird can travel as much as 6,000 kilometres (3,700 miles) from its breeding grounds as far north as Alaska to its wintering grounds in Mexico, and back again.

Some monarch butterflies will travel nearly 3,200 kilometres (2,000 miles) from summer range in Canada to winter range in Mexico, the Gulf states and southern California. In spring they will begin the return flight, mating and laying eggs as they go.

Very few of the butterflies make the full round trip back to their starting point. Most often, the final leg of the return journey is completed by their offspring.

In their wintering grounds the butterflies group together on tree branches for shared warmth on cool days, forming 'butterfly trees' which are huge masses of the insects. Some forest areas hold literally billions of

ABOVE Even the lowly earthworm has a lifespan that can range from a surprisingly long five to ten years.

RIGHT A herd of springbok grazes along an African hillside. Animals of this species at one time made up the greatest herds of animals ever recorded.

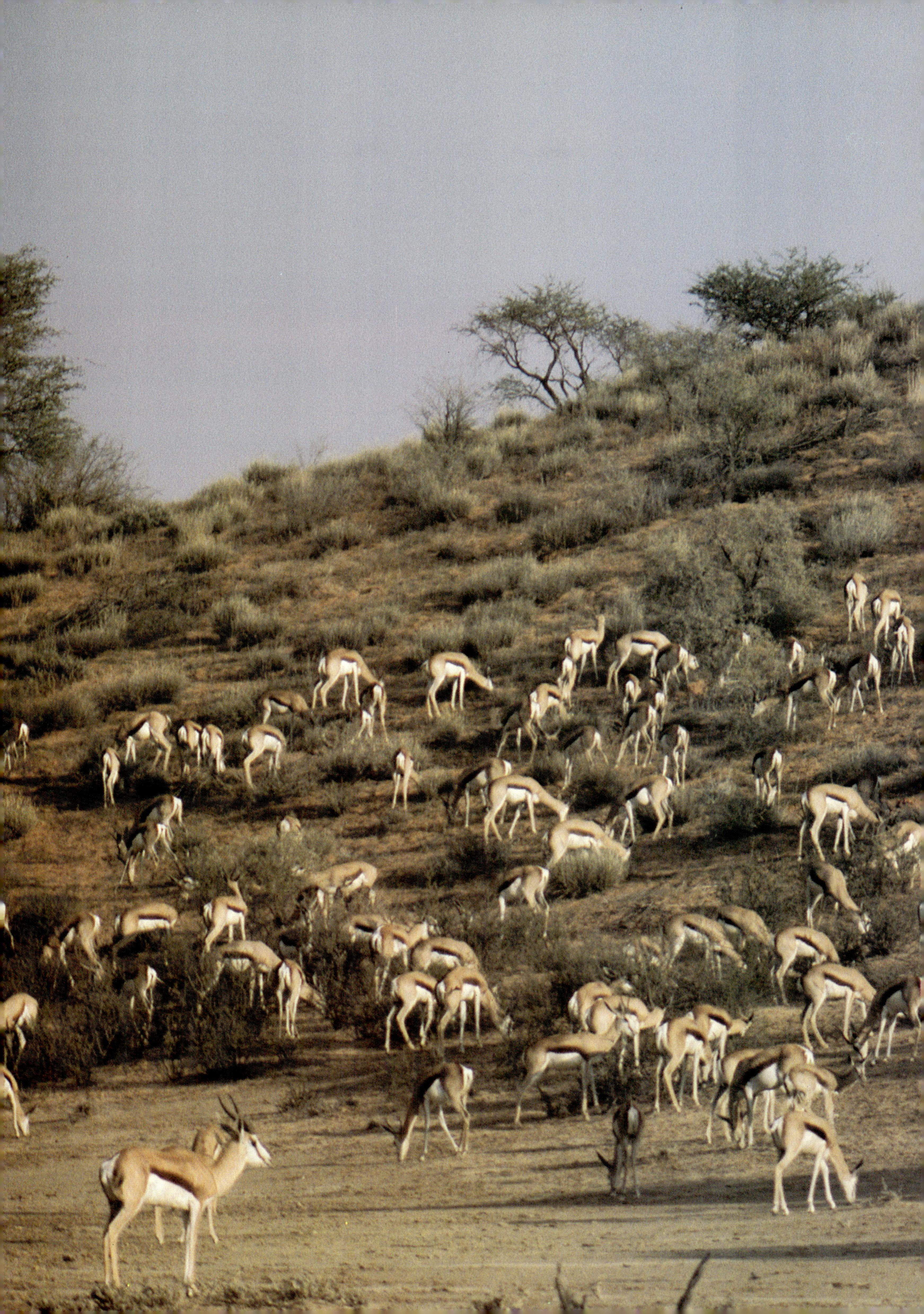

them at this time of the year. On warm days they might leave the trees temporarily, returning to roost for the night. They will begin to mate as the cold polar front begins to recede, generally near the end of February.

Not all of the monarchs migrate. Studies have shown that about a third of the butterflies that emerge in the Great Lakes region in late summer and early autumn will hibernate there in hollow trees while the other two-thirds make the traditional flight to the south.

A much larger migrant, the barren ground caribou of northern Canada, makes its annual sojourn in the opposite direction. From February to April small herds begin moving north towards the calving grounds around the Arctic Circle. About the first week in May they will converge into much larger herds – some as long as 320 kilometres (200 miles) – and begin the trek across the tundra. At this point, the nearest calving grounds lie at least 400 kilometres (250 miles) away. With the pregnant females leading the way, the herds will cover from 25 to 50 kilometres (15 to 30 miles) every day, crossing icy, swollen rivers under constant threat from predators.

Calves are born in May and June, and by July the herds begin to disperse to begin the return migration south to the forested areas. In August the travel begins again in earnest. By late September the herds have returned to their wintering grounds.

The 20-centimetre (8-inch) grunion, a fish native to the coastal waters of southern California, makes its annual sea-to-land 'run' in swarms of millions every two weeks from March through June. The small fish ride the peak waves of full-moon high tide onto the beach, where the female digs a hole in the sand and empties her swollen abdomen of eggs. The male, which wraps itself around the female, immediately fertilizes the eggs. As the next wave washes the beach, the grunion return to the sea. The process has taken less than a minute.

RIGHT *Before deliberate extermination efforts by the "white man", the bison ranged across most of North America in numbers estimated as high as 60 million.*

RIGHT *A common autumn and spring sight across much of North America are the V-shaped flocks of Canada geese migrating south in the autumn and back north in the spring.*

LEFT Some monarch butterflies travel from Canada to Mexico and vice versa on their autumn and spring migrations.

In the moist sand, the eggs incubate until the next high tide washes over that section of the beach. At that point the fry hatch, wiggle their way up through the sand and catch the receding waters for a ride out to sea.

At the other end of the time spectrum, some animals take even longer than a few months or a year to complete their full migration. The Atlantic salmon, which spawns in the rivers of North America and Europe, spends anywhere from one to eight years in fresh water before entering the ocean, where it will spend from one to four years before reaching sexual maturity and returning to fresh water to spawn.

During the 'run' upstream in the river, which covers as much as 19 kilometres (12 miles) a day, the males take on bright colouration and a hooked lower jaw. None of the salmon feed during the spawn, and an individual may lose as much as 25 percent of its body weight before reaching its 'home' waters where it was hatched. Experimental evidence strongly suggests that it is the smell or taste of the water that guides the fish back.

About a quarter of the fish will survive the 'run' to return downstream to the ocean, where they will spend four to eighteen months before starting on another spawning 'run'. Only an estimated 6 percent, however, will ever complete a second 'run'. Among the Pacific salmon, none of the fish survive the first spawning.

The common eel reverses the process of the salmon, breeding in the Sargasso Sea, southeast of Bermuda. After hatching, the larvae spend about a year in the water of the North Atlantic before entering the rivers of North America and Europe as small, transparent elvers, or glass eels. After six or seven years, the eels journey back to the Sargasso Sea and begin the cycle anew.

All common eels breed in salt water, including those that are landlocked in ponds and pools. Lacking a direct watery route to the ocean, this snakelike fish can wriggle over short spans of grass to reach nearby rivers. The thick skin and narrow gill slits of the eel help to prevent

LEFT The barren ground caribou of northern Canada annually moves to and from calving grounds around the Arctic Circle.

drying out during the overland trip. Eel ladders have been built in some countries where commercial fishing for the creatures is practised.

Reproduction is only one reason for large scale migration. According to popular myth, Norway's lemmings, are wont to run headlong into the oceans to their death. In fact, the communal journey of these small rodents are what is known as removal migration. Their purpose is to alleviate the pressure of burgeoning populations on the available food sources.

A female lemming can produce several litters of three to nine new offspring every year. This phenomenal rate of addition to the population can be enhanced by mild winters which allow more of the animals to survive.

For these reasons, the species will experience population explosions simultaneously over large areas. Entire mountainsides will see the numbers of the rodents increase far beyond the level that can survive there. As the young adults are pushed to and beyond the edges of the favourable habitat, some must eventually come to a habitat that simply will not support them. Their only choice is the removal migration, which seems to happen at three- or four-year intervals.

Suddenly thousands of young lemmings are moving down the mountainsides into and across the lowlands. Their short lives leave no time to waste in reaching their new habitat, so they run directly across open fields and through villages. They are strong swimmers and will generally continue right into those rivers and lakes where they can see the far shore. This is probably the origin of the folklore attached to them.

Whether running or swimming, they continue towards the highest ground in sight. When they finally arrive at the base of a mountain, they will begin climbing immediately. If one migration group moving up a mountain encounters another group moving down the same

LEFT Vast herds of gnu make their annual migration across Massai Mara in Kenya.

mountain, the climbers will run at right angles along the bottom of the valley until a marked decrease in the number of descenders is noticed. Although the migration puts lemmings under severe threat from predators, it also moves them to a more favourable habitat and a better chance of reproduction, which is the major force behind much animal activity.

The massive herds of zebra, wildebeeste and Thomson's gazelle of Africa's Serengeti Plains make regular migrations corresponding to the wet and dry seasons. The herds will spend the dry season in the thorn forests to the northwest and the wet season on the open plains. Serengeti National Park was created in 1929 expressly to protect the migration routes.

Army ants, unlike most of their cousins which have completely stationary nest sites, practise a form of removal migration every day during certain periods of the nest's cycle. Although the colony may number upwards of half-a-million ants, the insects unfailingly move the nest once a day during these times, and may relocate more than 8 kilometres (5 miles) during a two-month period. Any insect, small invertebrate or even larger animal that is unable to get out of the way of this relentless march is killed.

This migration is tied directly to the stage of development of the colony's current body. When the larvae finally pupate and no longer need to be fed immense quantities of food every day, the colony becomes stationary. A temporary nest is established. In a few days the queen lays a new batch of eggs, her body shrinks and she is once again able to walk on her own.

Now, as the larvae and their appetite grow, raiding trails might extend out from the nest more than 90 metres (300 feet). The workers are fighting a losing battle to keep the colony fed. Finally, no single site can provide enough food for more than a day, and the migration begins.

The colony moves every night to a new temporary nest site discovered that day by one of the raiding columns. The workers carry the young larvae in their mandibles. Each night's move may take six to nine hours.

The gossamer spider has a much easier time of it in its migration. Climbing to the top of a weed stalk, the spider sticks its abdomen into the air and shoots a length of silk from its spinnerets. As the wind tugs on the silk the spider extrudes more and more of it, until enough lift is created to support the spider's weight. Now the spider releases its hold on the plant and is carried by the wind. These animals, although totally terrestrial, have been found hundreds of miles from land.

Even the lowly earthworm goes through a migration of sorts. Daily it moves to the surface at night to feed and returns back underground to escape the light of day. In addition, if it encounters dry or cold soil it will move deeper into the soil, whereas if it runs into damp or warm soil it will migrate upwards.

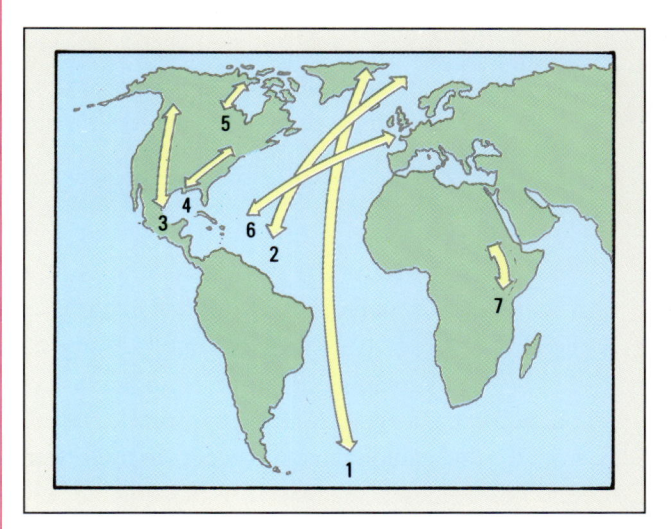

MIGRATION ROUTES

1 Arctic tern: North Pole to South Pole
2 blue whale: polar waters of Atlantic to tropical waters
3 Rufous humming bird: southern Alaska to Gulf of Mexico
4 monarch butterfly: Southern Canada (around Great Lakes) to Gulf of Mexico
5 barren grand caribou: Arctic Circle (the tree line)
6 common eel: rivers of northern Europe and northern North America to the Sarganso Sea
7 zebra, wildebeast and giraffe: Seregenti Plains (Africa) north west to the far side of the Seregenti National Park

LEFT More than three-quarters of Atlantic salmon on a given spawning run will die en route to their spawning grounds or soon after completing their mating rites.

At The Edge

Preceding chapters have taken a positive, marvelling, even joyful, look at the extraordinary animals of this planet; this one will be sad and pessimistic. It can be nothing else, for the animals in this case are extraordinary by virtue of having been pushed by man to the very edge of extinction.

Many of the animals on the following list may very well not be with us by the turn of the century. Some observers predict that the earth will lose fully one-fifth of all its species within 20 years. Untold numbers of species are expected to be lost even before we have learned of their existence.

Man has developed into too enterprising and aggressive an animal for the planet to support, unless he reins himself in. Our developments, our agricultural practices and our outright slaughter of other animals is simply more than these can withstand.

As you read these words, 20 hectares (50 acres) of rainforest are being destroyed, cut and burned to make way for totally inappropriate agriculture. The farms that will occupy the space when the lush vegetation and all native animal species are gone will survive only a few years. The vast majority of the rainforest nutrients are held in the vegetation. At best, the soil is poor and will support man's crops for only the very short term. Then, when the current site has failed, the peasant farmer will

RIGHT *The luxurious coat of the leopard has been the downfall of the animal, making it a prime target for the world's illegal animal trade.*

RIGHT *The snow leopard is just one of hundreds of animals teetering at the edge of extinction.*

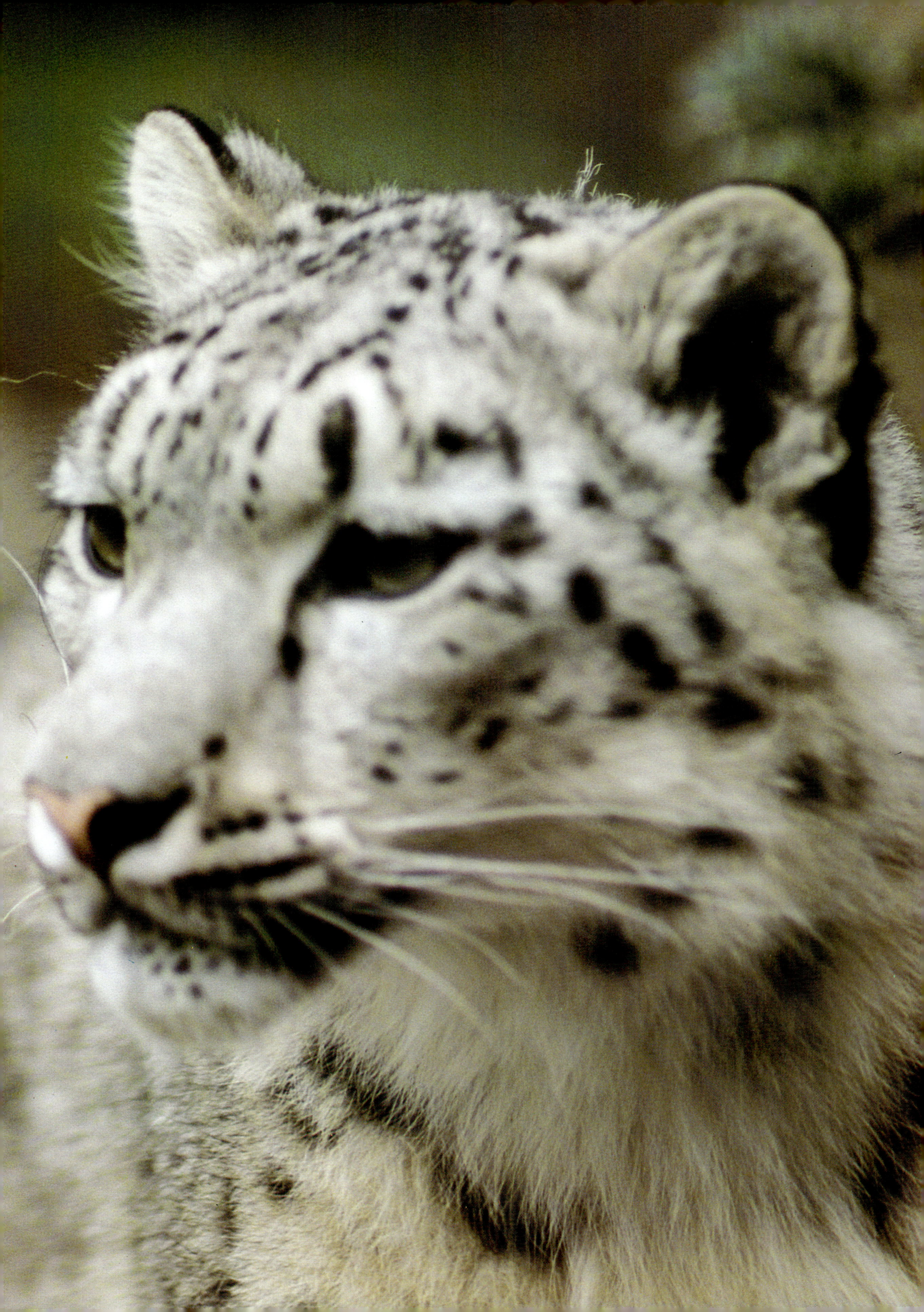

attack the next nearest section of rainforest to carve out another sure-to-fail farm.

The earth has about 81 million hectares (2 billion acres) of rainforest left, about 7 percent of the total land mass. Within those ecosystems live about half of all living species.

More direct attacks on animals are also taking their toll. The world now supports a $1.5 billion (about £96 million) per year illegal trade in animals and animal parts. This underground market involves almost any creature that someone is willing to pay enough money for, but some species have been harder hit than others. Many species of the big cats have been placed on the list below for their beautiful furs.

In the past 10 years poachers, often armed with automatic weapons, have reduced the world's population of elephants from more than 1.3 million to fewer than 400,000. Elephant tusk ivory sells for about $100 (about £64) per pound. The carcass of the slaughtered animal is usually left to rot.

The world's entire population of the amazing rhinoceros has been gunned down to leave perhaps 7,000 animals, including all sub-species everywhere. A single

ABOVE *Rhinos, such as this black rhino, have been reduced to about 7,000 in the entire world today through poaching for their horns, which sell for as much as £6,500 ($10,000) each to be made into dagger hilts for oil-rich Arabs in Yemen.*

rhino horn can sell for as much as $10,000 (about £6,410). It may be used as a decorative dagger hilt for some oil-rich Arab in Yemen. Again, the poachers have no use for the massive carcass.

The developed world is no less guilty of such destruction. In the few hundred years that European peoples have lived in North America, they have wiped out more than 70 animal species and pushed many, such as the Florida panther, so close to the brink of extinction that they are almost certainly doomed.

The following list of endangered species comes from the United States Fish & Wildlife Service. Because placement on the list involves a drawn-out bureaucratic process, and there exists a lengthy waiting list of species for consideration, this is one of the more conservative compilations of animals on the brink. The lists of some other organizations, such as the International Union for the Conservation of Nature and Natural Resources and the International Council for Bird Preservation, include many additional species. We chose the Fish & Wildlife Service because it is the most wide-ranging and offers the best idea of the magnitude of the situation.

ABOVE The distinctive shape of the elephant skull. The discovery of scattered bones often indicates a 'natural' death, but in the case of elephants and rhinos it may also point to a violent end at the hands of poachers, who strip their quarry of its valuable ivory, leaving the massive carcass to rot.

The Indian python is one of the few reptiles that have made it to the list of endangered species. Those furred and feathered creatures, with more appeal to most humans, seem to have an easier time of making the list.

Appendix

The following list of endangered species comes from the United States Fish & Wildlife Service. Because placement on the list involves a drawn-out bureaucratic process, and there exists a lengthy waiting list of species for consideration, this is one of the more conservative compilations of animals on the brink. The lists of some other organizations, such as the International Union for the Conservation of Nature and Natural Resources and the International Council for Bird Preservation, include many additional species. We chose the Fish & Wildlife Service because it is the most wide-ranging and offers the best idea of the magnitude of the situation.

MAMMALS

A Lowland anoa, mountain anoa, giant sable antelope, argali, giant armadillo, African wild ass, Asian wild ass, avahi, aye-aye

B babirusa, barred bandicoot, desert bandicoot, lesser rabbit bandicoot, pig-footed bandicoot, Bulmer's fruit bat, bumblebee bat, grey bat, Hawaiian hoary bat, Indiana bat, little Mariana fruit bat, Mariana fruit bat, Mexican long-nosed bat, Ozark big-eared bat, Rodriguez fruit bat, Sanborn's long-nosed bat, Virginia big-eared bat, Baluchistan bear, brown bear (Tibet, Italy), beaver (Mongolia), wood bison, bobcat (Central America), bontebok,

C bactrian camel, Andean cat, black-footed cat, flat-headed cat, Iriomote cat, leopard cat, marbled cat, Pakistan sand cat, golden cat, tiger cat, Apennine chamois, cheetah, chinchilla, Malabar large-spotted civet, cochito, eastern cougar,

D bactrian deer, Barbary deer, Bawean deer, Cedros Island mule deer, Colombian white-tailed deer, Corsican red deer, Eld's brow-antlered deer, Formosan sika deer, hog deer, key deer, marsh deer, McNeill's deer, musk deer, North China sika deer, pampas deer, Persian fallow deer. Philippine deer, Ryukyu sika deer, Shansi sika deer, South China sika deer, swamp deer, Visayan deer, dhole (Asian wild dog), dibbler, African wild dog, drill, dugong, Jentink's duiker

E western giant eland, African elephant, Asian elephant

F black-footed ferret, northern swift fox, San Joaquin kit fox, Simien fox

G Arabian gazelle, Clark's gazelle, Cuvier's gazelle, Mhorr gazelle, Moroccan gazelle, Pelzein's gazelle, Rio de Oro Dama gazelle, sand gazelle, Arabian Peninsula gazelle, slender-horned gazelle, Gibbon, wild goat, goral, gorilla

H hispid hare, Swayne's hartebeest, Tora hartebeest, pygmy hog, Przewalski's horse, huemul, hutia, Barbary hyena, brown hyena

I Pyrenean ibex, Walia ibex, impala, indri

J jaguar, jaguarundi

K Tasmanian forester kangaroo, kouprey

L capped langur, Douc langur, entellus langur, Francois langur, golden langur, Pagi Island langur, Lemur, clouded leopard, snow leopard, spotted linsang, Asian lion, Spanish lynx

M lion-tailed macaque, Amazonian manatee, Florida manatee, mandrill, Tana River mangabey, white-collared mangabey, margay, markhor, buff-headed marmoset, buffy tufted-ear marmoset, cotton-top marmoset, Goeldi's marmoset, Vancouver Island marmot, eastern jerboa marsupial, marsupial-mouse, Formosan yellow-throated marten, black colobus monkey, Diana monkey, howler monkey, L'hoest's monkey, Preuss' red colobus monkey, proboscis monkey, red-backed squirrel monkey, red-bellied monkey, red-eared nose-spotted monkey, spider monkey, Tana River red colobus monkey, woolly spider monkey, yellow-tailed woolly monkey, Zanzibar red colobus monkey, Alabama beach mouse, Australian native mouse, Choctawhatchee beach mouse, Field's mouse, Gould's mouse, Key Largo cotton mouse, New Holland mouse, Perdido Key beach mouse, salt marsh harvest mouse, Shark Bay mouse, Shortridge's mouse, smoky mouse, western mouse, Fea's muntjac,

N eastern native-cat, numbat

O ocelot, orang-utan, Arabian oryx;
Cameroon clawless otter, long-tailed otter, giant otter,
marine otter, southern river otter

P giant panda, pangolin, Florida panther, planiglae,
thin-spined porcupine, Leadbeater's possum,
mountain pygmy possum, scaly-tailed possum,
Mexican prairie dog, peninsular pronghorn,
Sonoran pronghorn, pudu, puma

Q quokka

R Ryukyu rabbit, volcano rabbit, false water rat,
Fresno kangaroo rat, giant kangaroo rat,
Morro Bay kangaroo rat, Stephens' kangaroo rat,
stick-nest rat, Tipton kangaroo rat, rat-kangaroo,
black rhinoceros, great Indian rhinoceros,
Javan rhinoceros, northern white rhinoceros,
Sumutran rhinoceros

S Mongolian saiga, southern bearded saki,
white-nosed saki, Caribbean monk seal,
Hawaiian monk seal, Mediterranean monk seal,
seledang (guar), serow, Barbary serval, shapo, shou,
siamang, sifakas, three-toed sloth, Cuban solenodon,
Haitian solenodon, Carolina northern flying squirrel,
Delmarva Peninsula fox squirrel,
Mount Graham red squirrel,
Virginia northern flying squirrel, Barbary stag,
Kashmir stag, Zanzibar suni

T Arabian tahr, tamaraw, golden-rumped tamarin,
pied tamarin, Asian tapir, Brazilian tapir,
Central American tapir, mountain tapir. tiger,
Tasmanian tiger

U uakari, urial

V vicuûa, Amargosa vole, Hualapai Mexican vole,

W banded hare wallaby, brindled nail-tailed wallaby,
crescent nail-tailed wallaby, Parma wallaby,
western hare wallaby, yellow-footed rock wallaby,
blue whale, bowhead whale, finback whale,
humpback whale, right whale, Sei whale, sperm whale,
maned wolf, red wolf, hairy-nosed wombat,
Key Largo woodrat

Y wild yak

Z mountain zebra

BIRDS

A Hawaii akepa, Maui akepa, Kauai akialoa,
Akiapolaau, short-tailed albatross

B yellow-shouldered blackbird, masked bobwhite,
Abbott's booby, western bristlebird,
western rufous bristlebird, Guam broadbill,
Mauritius Olivaceous bulbul; Sïo Miguel bullfinch,
New Zealand bushwren, great Indian bustard

C cahow, Andean condor, Californian condor,
Hawaiian coot, banded cotinga, white-winged cotinga,
black-necked crane, Cuba sandhill crane, hooded crane,
Japanese crane, Mississippi sandhill crane,
Siberian white crane, white-naped crane, whooping
crane, Hawaii creeper, Molokai creeper, Oahu creeper,
Hawaiian crow, Mariana crow, Mauritius cuckoo-shrike,
Réunion cuckoo-shrike, razor-billed curassow,
red-billed curassow, Trinidad white-headed curassow,
Eskimo curlew

D cloven-feathered dove, Grenada gray-fronted dove,
Hawaiian duck, Laysan duck, pink-headed duck,
white-winged wood duck

E bald eagle, Greenland white-tailed eagle,
harpy eagle, Philippine monkey-eating eagle,
Spanish imperial eagle, Chinese egret

F American peregrine falcon,
Eurasian peregrine falcon, northern aplomado falcon,
Laysan finch, Nihoa finch, Euler's flycatcher,
Seychelles paradise flycatcher, Tahiti flycatcher,
Seychelles fody, Andrew's frigate bird,

G Aleutian Canada goose, Hawaiian goose,
Christmas Island goshawk, slender-billed grackle,
Eyrean grasswren, Atitlan grebe, Nordmann's greenshank,
horned guan, Audouin's gull, relict gull

H Anjouan Island sparrow hawk, Galapagos hawk,
Hawaiian hawk, hook-billed hermit,
crested honeycreeper, helmeted honeycreeper

I Japanese crested ibis

J kagu, kakapo, Mauritius kestrel, Seychelles kestrel,
Guam Micronesian kingfisher, Cuba hook-billed kite,
Everglade snail kite, Grenada hook-billed kite, kokako

K glaucous macaw, indigo macaw, little blue macaw,
Seychelles magpie-robin, red-faced malkoha,
Mariana mallard, Maleo megapode,
Micronesian megapode, Nihoa miller bird,
Hawaiian common moorhen,
Mariana common moorhen,

N Puerto Rican nightjar, nukupu'u

O Kauai O'o, Arabian ostrich, West African ostrich,

O'u, Anjouan scops owl, giant scops owl,
Seychelles owl, Morden's owlet

P palila, Forbes' parakeet, golden parakeet,
golden-shouldered parakeet, Mauritius parakeet,
ochre-marked parakeet, orange-bellied parakeet,
paradise parakeet, scarlet-chested parakeet,
turquoise parakeet, Australian parrot, Cuban parrot,
ground parrot, imperial parrot, Puerto Rican parrot,
red-browned parrot, red-capped parrot,
red-necked parrot, red-spectacled parrot,
St. Lucia parrot, thick-billed parrot,
vinaceous-breasted parrot, Maui parrotbill,
brown pelican, Galapagos penguin, Hawaiian dark-
rumped petrel, bar-tailed pheasant,
Blyth's tragopan pheasant, brown eared pheasant,
Cabot's tragopan pheasant, Chinese monal pheasant,
Edward's pheasant, Elliot's pheasant, imperial pheasant,
Mikado pheasant, Palawan peacock pheasant,
Sclater's monal pheasant, Swinhole's pheasant,
western tragopan pheasant, white eared pheasant,
Azores wood pigeon, Chatham Island pigeon,
Mindoro zone-tailed pigeon, Puerto Rican plain pigeon,
black-fronted piping-guan, Koch's pitta,
New Zealand shore plover, po'ouli,
Attwater's greater prairie-chicken,

Q Merriam's Montezuma quail, resplendent quetzal,

R Aukland Island rail, California clapper rail,
Guam rail, light-footed clapper rail,
Lord Howe wood rail, Yuma clapper rail, Darwin's rhea,
Chatham Island robin, scarlet-breasted robin,
grey-necked rockfowl, white-necked rockfowl,
long-tailed ground roller

S noisy scrub-bird, Cebu black shama,
San Clemente loggerhead shrike, red siskin,
Cape Sable seaside sparrow,
Florida grasshopper sparrow, Ponape mountain starling,
Rothschild's starling, Hawaiian stilt, oriental white stork,
wood stork, Mariana grey swiftlet,

T Campbell Island flightless teal, Califonia least tern,
white-breasted thrasher, large Kauai thrush,
Molokai thrush, New Zealand thrush,
small Kauai thrush, solitary tinamou,
Martinique trembler

V black-capped vireo, least Bell's vireo,

W plain wanderer, Bachman's warbler,
Barbados yellow warbler, Kirtland's warbler,
Rodriquez warbler, Semper's warbler,
Seychelles warbler, western whipbird,
bridled white-eye, Norfolk Island white-eye,

Ponape greater white-eye, Seychelles white-eye,
imperial woodpecker, ivory-billed woodpecker,
red-cockaded woodpecker, Tristam's woodpecker,
Guadeloupe house wren, St. Lucia house wren

REPTILES

A Chinese alligator, Culebra Island giant anole

B Jamaican boa, Puerto Rican boa, Round Island boa,
Virgin Islands tree boa

C Apaporis River caiman, black caiman,
broad-snouted caiman, Yacare caiman,
San Esteban Island chuckwalla, African dwarf crocodile,
African slender-snouted crocodile, American crocodile,
Ceylon mugger crocodile, Congo dwarf crocodile,
Cuban crocodile, Morelet's crocodile,
mugger crocodile, Nile crocodile, Orinoco crocodile,
saltwater crocodile, Siamese crocodile

G gavial, day gecko, Monito gecko,
Round Island day gecko

I Anegada ground iguana, Barrington land iguana,
Fiji banded iguana, Fiji crested iguana,
Grand Cayman ground iguana, Jamaican iguana,
Waiting Island ground iguana

L blunt-nosed leopard lizard, Hierro giant lizard,
St. Croix ground lizard

M Bengal monitor, Komodo Island monitor
(Komodo dragon), yellow monitor

P Indian python

S San Francisco garter snake

T tartaruga, river terrapin, tomistoma,
angulated tortoise, Bolson tortoise, Galapagos tortoise,
radiated tortoise, tracaja, tuatara,
Alabama red-bellied turtle, aquatic box turtle,
black softshell turtle, Burmese peacock turtle,
Central American river turtle,
Cuatro Cienegas softshell turtle, geometric turtle,
green sea turtle, hawksbill sea turtle,
Indian sawback turtle, Indian softshell turtle,
Kemp's ridley sea turtle, leatherback sea turtle,
peacock softshell turtle, Plymouth red-bellied turtle,
western swamp turtle, spotted pond turtle,
three-keeled Asia turtle

V Lar Valey viper

AMPHIBIANS

F Israeli painted frog, Panamanian golden frog,
Stephen Island frog,

S Chinese giant salamander,
desert slender salamander, Japanese giant salamander,
Santa Cruz long-toed salamander,
Texas blind salamander, African viviparous toad,
Cameroon toad, Houston toad, Monte Verde toad,
Wyoming toad

FISHES

A Ala Balik, ayumodoki,

B Mexican blindcat, Asian bonytongue

C Thailand catfish, giant catfish, Alabama cavefish,
bonytail chub, Borax Lake chub, humpback chub,
Mohave tui chub, Owens tui chub, Pahranagat chub,
Yaqui chub, cicek, cui-ui

D Ash Meadows dace, Kendall Warm Springs dace,
moapa dace, amber darter, boulder darter,
fountain darter, Maryland darter, Okaloosa darter,
watercress darter

G Big Bend gambusia, Clear Creek gambusia,
Pecos gambusia, San Marcos gambusia

K Pahrump killifish

L Conasauga longperch

M Scioto madtom, Smoky madtom

N nekogigi

P Ash Meadows Amargosa pupfish,
Comanche Springs pupfish, desert pupfish,
Devils Hole pupfish, Leon Springs pupfish,
Owens pupfish, Warm Springs pupfish

S Cape Fear shiner, White River spinedace,
Hiko White River springfish, Railroad Valley springfish,
Colorado squawfish, Unarmoured threespine stickleback,
shortnose sturgeon, June sucker, Lost River sucker,
Modoc sucker, shortnose sucker

T Miyako tango, Ikan temolek, Gila topminnow,
totoaba, Gila trout

W woundfin

SNAILS

S Iowa Pleistocene snail, Manus Island tree snail,
Oahu tree snail, Virginia fringed mountain snail

CLAMS

M Curtus' mussel, Judge Tait's mussel,
Marshall's mussel, penitent mussel,
Louisiana pearlshell, Alabama lamp pearly mussel,
Appalachian monkeyface pearly mussel,
birdwing pearly mussel,
Cumberland bean pearly mussel,
Cumberland monkeyface pearly mussel,
Curtis' pearly mussel, dromedary pearly mussel,
green-blossom pearly mussel,
Higgins' eye pearly mussel,
little-wing pearly mussel, Nicklin's pearly mussel,
orange-footed pearly mussel, pale lilliput pearly mussel,
pink mucket pearly mussel, Tampico pearly mussel,
tubercled-blossom pearly mussel,
turgid-blossom pearly mussel,
white cat's paw pearly mussel,
white wartyback pearly mussel,
yellow-blossom pearly mussel

P fine-rayed pigtoe, rough pigtoe, shiny pigtoe,
fat pocketbook

S tan riffle shell, James River spinymussel,
Tar River spinymussel, stirrup shell

CRUSTACEANS

A Hay's Spring amphipod

C Cambarus zophonastes crayfish, Nashville crayfish,
Shasta crayfish

I Socorro isopod

S Alabama cave shrimp, California freshwater shrimp,
Kentucky cave shrimp

INSECTS

B Kretschmarr Cave mould beetle,
Tooth Cave ground beetle, El Segundo blue butterfly,
Lange's metalmark butterfly, lotus blue butterfly,
mission blue butterfly, Palos Verdes blue butterfly,
San Bruno elfin butterfly, Schaus swallowtail butterfly,
Smith's blue butterfly

ARACHNIDS

H Bee Creek Cave harvestman

P Tooth Cave pseudoscorpion

S Tooth Cave spider

Further Reading

The following books provide additional insight into the extraordinary life that inhabits this planet:

ALEXANDER, R.M. Elastic Mechanisms in Animal Movement. *1988. Cambridge University Press.*
BAKER, R. ROBIN. The Evolutionary Ecology of Animal Migration. *1978. Holmes & Meier.*
BARNARD, C.J. Animal Behavior: Ecology & Evolution. *1983. Wiley.*
BRIGHT, MICHAEL. Animal Language. *1985. Cornell University Press.*
BURGESS, ROBERT. Secret Languages of the Sea. *1982. Putnam Publishing Group.*
BURTON, MAURICE & BURTON, JANE. The Colorful World of Animals. *1979. Smith Publishers.*
CALDER, WILLIAM A., III. Size, Function & Life History. *1984. Harvard University Press.*
CHINERY, MICHAEL, ED. Dictionary of Animals. *1984. Arco.*
DAVIS, SIMON J. The Archaeology of Animals. *1987. Yale Univeristy Press.*
DILLON, LAWRENCE S. Animal Variety: An Evolutionary Account. *1980. William C. Brown.*
HANSELL, MICHALE H. Animal Architecture & Building Behavior. *1984. Longman.*
HEADSTROM, RICHARD. Weird & Beautiful. *1984. Associated University Press.*
HOWELL, ALFRED B. Speed in Animals, Their Specialization for Running & Leaping. *1965. Hafner.*
MATSUDA, RYUICHI. Animal Evolution in Changing Environments: With Special Reference to Abnormal Metamorphosis. *1987. Wiley.*
MUYBRIDGE, EDWARD. Animals in Motion. *1957. Dover.*
PENNY, MALCOLM. Animal Defenses. *1988. Bookwright Press.*
SEDDON, TONY. Animal Movement. *1988. Facts on File.*
SILVERSTIEN, ALVIN & SILVERSTEIN, VIRGINIA. Nature's Living Lights: Fireflies & Other Bioluminescent Creatures. *1988. Little.*
WATERMAN, TALBOT H. Animal Navigation. *1988. W.H. Freeman.*

Index

Numbers in italics refer to illustrations

A
adaptive radiation, 13, 15
albatross, royal, 75
alligator, 108
alpaca, 6
anaconda, 26, 65
angler fish, 69, 75–6
Ankole cattle, 38
Anopheles, 57
anteaters (spiny): reproduction of echidna, 70, 72–3; tongues, 35, 37
antelope, 38; klipspringer, 63; pronghorn, 6, *9*, 60
antlers, *34*, *36*, 38
ants, 39, 94, 107, 109; army, 115
apes, 76
aphids, 107
arachnids, 26, 123
archerfish, 69
armadillo, 42; bony plates covering, 42, *43*; giant, 42
Arthropoda, 15

B
badger, European, 101
barracuda, 60
bats, 60–1; flight, 60–1, *63*; fruit, 6; hunting by 'bounced' sound, 69, *69*; kalong, 61; Kitti's hog-nosed, 61; long-winged, 60; noctule, 60; speed, 60; vampire, 57
bears, 25–6; Asian sloth, 57; attacks on man by, 57; black, 57; brown *24*, 25–6, 57, 77, *77*; hibernation, 104, *106*, 107; polar (white), 26, 57; reproduction, 77, *77*
beaver, 26, 75, 88–93, *88–9*, *91*
bee-eater, African, 98
bees, 39; honeybees, *14*, 60, *61*, *92–3*, 93–4
beetles 39; Goliath 26; hairy-winged dwarf, 26
Berardius, 62
billfishes, 31
bills, 37–8
bioluminescence, 69, *69*
bird nests, 98–101
birds of prey, 65
bison, 11, 38, 109, *112*
blue whale, 9, 16, 18, 60, 62–3, 110; diet, 102; northern, 18; pygmy, 18; southern, 18
boa constrictor, 65
boobie, blue-footed, *12*
bowerbird, 82; brown, 82; golden, 82; mating colouration, 82; satin, 82
buffalo, 38; horns, 38; Indian, 38; Texas longhorn, 38; water, *35*
Bufo marinus, 84
butterfly: back to front, 85; glass-winged, 87; migration, 110, 112, *113*; milkweed, 49–50; mimicking by, *79*, 85; monarch, *48*, 49–50, *79*, 85, 110, 112, *113*; Queen Alexandra birdwing, 27
butterfly fish, 85

C
camel, 8; water loss, 104, *105*
camouflage and disguise, 78, *80*, 81, *81*, 85, 87, *87*, 97
capybara, 26, *26*
caribou, 6, 112, *114*
castlebuilder, rufous-breasted, 98
cat, 65; house, 60, 65
caterpillars, 39, 85; stick-, 85
catfish, *50*
centipede, 39
chameleon: changing colour, 78, *78*; dwarf, 35; eyes, *29*, 39; Meller's, *29*, *33*; Oustalet's, 35; tongue, *33*, 35, 37
cheetah, 58, *58*
chimpanzee, *13*, 75, 107
chiton, 42
Chordata, 15
clams, 15, 123; European freshwater, 108; giant, 21; *Tindaria callistiformis*, 77
co-adaptation, 13, *14*
cobra, 75; king, 44–5; spitting, 45
cockroach, 11; Oriental, 109
colouration, colour changes, 40, 78–87; camouflage and disguise, 78, *80*, 81, *81*, 85, 87, *87*; mating, 81–2, *83*, *84*; mimicry, 52, 78, *79*, 85; trickery, 85; warning, *84*, 84–5
condor, Andean, 108
copilia, 38
cougar (mountain lion), 57, 63, 65
coyote, 75
crab, 15; blue, 76–7; grenadier, 44; hermit, 44, *46*, 107; masking, 85
crocodile, 11; Congo dwarf, 26; saltwater, 26
cuttlefish, colour changes, 78

D
Darwin, Charles, 9, 11, *12*, 13
deer, 22, 38, 39; antlers, *34*, 38; fallow, *34*; mouse, 22; mule, 6; musk, 38; red, 8; white-tailed, 6, 6, *80*, 81
diet, 102–7

dinosaurs, 11, 16
diplodocus, 16
dippers, 39
diseases transmitted by small animals, 56, 57
dolphin, 60, 69
dragonfly, 60; compound eyes of, *37*, 38

E
eagle, bald, 75, 98
earthworm, 109, *109*, 115
echidna (spiny anteater), reproduction, 70, 72–3
eel: American, 108; common, 113–114; electric, 50, *50*
electricity-generation, 50, *50*, 52
Electrophorus electricus, 50
elephant, 8, *16*, 16–18, 45, 57, 60; African, *17*, 18, 32, 104; Asian, 18, *28*, 32, 75, 108; diet, 104, *104*; Fenykoevi, 18; hearing, 67, 68; Jumbo, 18; longevity, 108; reproduction, 75, 76; trunk, 28, 30; tusks, *16*, 32, *32*
elephant bird, 22
elk, 6, 8, 38; mating, 70, *70*
endangered species, list of, 120–3
evolutionary theory, 9–15
eyes, *29*, *37*, *38*, 38–9

F
fangs, 46
feathers, *37*, 38
feigning death, 40–2
finch, 9, 75; weaver, 98
firefly, bioluminescence of, 69, *69*
fisher, 43
flea, 63; snow, 109; water, 107
flounder, 38
fly: housefly, 60, 109; robber, 27
flyers, non-avian, 60–2, *63*–4
flying dragon, 61–2
flying fish, 60, 62
fowl, mallee, 98
fox, grey, 60
frigate bird, mating colouration of, 81, *83*
frog, 63; African grey tree, 100; arrow-poison, 49, 84
frogmouth, 85, 87

G
Gaboon viper, fangs of, 46, *46*
gazelle, 8, *57*, 60; Thomson's, 115
geese, Canada, 110, *112*
gestation rates, 75
gila monster, 46, 49
giraffe, 8, *10*, *19*, *20*, 22, 75
Glaucus atlanticus, 44

gnu, migration of, *114*
goldfinch, colour changes, 81
goldfish, 60
gorilla, *23*, 25, 108
grasshopper, 84; shorthorn, 84
greyhound, 60
groundhog (woodchuck), *107*
grunion, 112

H
hamster, 75; golden, 75
hare, snowshoe, *80*, 81
hatchet fish, 69
hawk: duck, 58; red-shouldered, *67*; red-tailed, 67
hearing, 67, 68
heat-sensing organs, 59
hedgehog, spines of, 44, *45*
herbivores, 6, *6*, 8, 9, 10
heron, great blue, 75
hibernation, 104, *106*, 107, 112
hippopotamus, 104, *107*
honeybee, *14*, 60, *61*, *92–3*, 93–4
horns, *35*, 38
housefly, 60, 109
hummingbird: bee, 22, 76, 98; eggs, 76; feathers, *37*, 38; ruby-throated, 75; rufous, migration of, 110; speed, 60; Verrain, 76

I
induced ovulators, 77
infrasound, 67, *68*
insects, 15, 26–7, 38, 123; numbers of, 109; stick, 26

J
jack rabbit, 60, 63; blacktail, *66*
jaguar, 57
jellyfish, 44
jumping and leaping, 63, 65–6

K
kalong (fruit bat), 61
kangaroo, 9, 13; red, 26, 57, 63
kangaroo rat, 65
kingdoms, animal, 15
klipspringer, 63
koala, diet, 102, *102*
Komodo dragon, 26
krill, 16, 102

L
lantern-eye fish, 39
leaf fish, 87
lemming, 109; removal migration of, 114–115
lemurs, 8, 13; flying, 61
leopard, *116*; man-eating, 57;

snow, *117*
lifespan, 108–9, *109*
lion, 26, *53*, 77; attacks on man by, 57; camouflage, 87, *87*; cougar or mountain, 57, 63, *65*
lizards, 26; flying dragon, 61–2; gila monster, 46, 49; Komodo dragon, 26; Mexican bearded, 46, 49; moloch, 44; poisonous, 46, 49
llama, 6
lobster, 39, 108

M

mackerel, Atlantic, 75
macrotermes, 94
malaria, 57
mandrill, mating colouration, 82
marsupials, 9, 13, 26, 40, 57, 102
mating, 43–4, 69, *70*, 70–7, 78, 81, 97; colouration, 81–2, *83, 84*
migration, 109, 110–115; removal, 114–115
milkweed, *48*, 49–50, 85
millipedes, 39, 42
mimicry, 52, 78, *79*, 85
moa, 22
mockingbird, 9
mole, star-nosed, 31, *31*
mole rat, 38
Mollusca, 15
moloch ('thorny devil'), 44
mongoose, 45–6
monkey, proboscis, 32
moose, 6, *21*, 22; antlers of, *36*, 38
monotremes, 72
mormyrids (elephant-noses), *30*, 30–1
mosquito, 109
moth: Atlas silk, *27*; hawk, 60; Hercules emperor, *27*; noctuid, 67; peppered, 85; pug, 85
mouse: dormouse, 101; harvest, 101; hearing, 67; house, 75; meadow, 76
mouse deer, 22
muskox, 8
mussels, edible, 76

N

narwhal, 32
natural selection, theory of, 9, 11
nematocysts, 44
nightjar, 87
night vision, 65
nose, 30–2

O

octopus, 15, 39; blue-ringed, 49; colour changes, 78; venomous, 49
opossum, Virginia: diet, 102, *103*; feigning death, 40, *41*, 42; reproduction, *71*, 73, 75
osprey, *98*
ostrich, 22, *22*, *51*, 56, 60, 75; eggs, *74*, 76
owl, 60; barred, *100*

P

pangolin, 35, 37, 42
panther, Florida, 7
passenger pigeon, 109
Patu marplesi (spider), 26
pauropods, 39
peacock, mating colouration, *84*
Pearl of Laotze, 21
penguin: emperor, 75, 100; king, 100
pheasant, ring-necked, 75
Phoenix fowl, 38
pigeons, 67; passenger, 109
pill bug, *42*
pipefish, 75
piranha, attacks on man by, *52*, 57
plague, bubonic, *56*, 57
platypus (duck-bill), 28, 30, 50; reproduction, 70, 72
poison/venom, 44–50, 84–5, *85, 86*
'playing possum', 40–2
polecat, 52
porcupine, 42–4; mating, 43–4; North American, 42; quills of, 42–3, *44*
porcupine fish, 44
Portuguese man-of-war, 44
prairie dog, 101, *101*
praying mantis, 87
ptarmigan, camouflage, 81, *81*
pudu, 22, 38
puffers, 27
python, 65

Q

quelea, red-bellied, 109

R

rabbit, 65; cottontail, 38, *39*; eyes, 38, *39*
rabies, 58
rail, 22
rat, 46; crested, 85; kangaroo, 65; mole, 38; Norway, 56; plague transmitted by, *56*, 57
rattlesnake, 65; blacktailed, *59*; eastern diamond, *47*
raven, *98*
ray, 31, 38; oceanic, 77; torpedo, 50, 52
reindeer, 8
reproduction, 11, *70*, 70–7, 78, 113–14
reptiles, 22, 26, 72
rhinoceros, 57; black, *56*; courtship dance, 76; reproduction, 75, 76, *76*
robin, American, 60, *100*
rodents, 26, *56*, 88

S

sailfish, 60
salamander, fire, *84*; giant, 108
salmon, Atlantic, spawning run of, 113, *115*
sawfish, 31, 32

sea anemone, 44, 107, 108
sea horse, 75
sea slug, 85, *86*
sea snake, 44, 45
sea wasp, 44
seal: elephant, 32; harp, 63; Weddell, 63
shark, 21; attacks on man by, 55, 57–8; great white, 57; grey nurse, 57; hammerhead, 57; mako, 57; requiem, 57; sand-, 57; tiger, 57
shells/scales, protective, *40, 42, 42, 44, 46*
shrew, 25; hero, 25; musk, 22, 25
shrimp, 39
sight/vision, 65
size of animals, 9, 16–27, 40
skimmer bird: African, 37; black, 37; Indian, 37; lower bill of, 37–8
skunk: stink emitted by, *51*, 52, 54; warning colouration, *84*, 84
sloth, three-toed, 60, *60*
smells, emission of bad, *51*, 52
snails, 15, 39, *64*, 109, 123
snakes, 26, 44–6, 60, *62*, 107; anaconda, 26, 65; black-tailed rattlesnake, *59*; boa constrictor, 65; cobra, 44–5; coral, 52, 85, *85*; diamond rattlesnake, *47*; eastern garter, *62*; Gaboon viper, 46, *46*; heat-sensitive organs, 65; hognosed, *40*, 42; milk, 52, 85, *85*; mimicking colouration, 52, 85, *85*; moccasin, 65; pit viper, 65; python, 65; venomous, 44–6, 49
snow flea, 109
snow leopard, *117*
snowshoe hare, *80*, 81
sole, 38
speed of animals, 58, *58*, 60, *61*
spiders, 15, 26–7, 39, 94, 97–8; bird-eating, 26; black widow, *49*; Brazilian wandering, 46; camouflage, 87; gossamer, 115; hunting, 39; orb-weaving, 26–7, *95*, 97; purse-web, 97; trapdoor, 97–8; venomous, 46, 49; water, 98
spider's webs, 26–7, 94, *95*, 97–8
spines and quills, 42–4, 44–5, 49
sponges, 108
springbok, 109, *111*
springtail, 109
squid: colour changes, 78; giant, *18*, 21, 38
squirrel: 'flying', *64*; grey, 75
starfish, 39; eyes of, 38, *38*
stick-caterpillar, 85
stick insects, 26
stickleback, 100–1
stinging cells, 44, 49
stonefish, 49
sturgeon, 108
sunfish, 76
swan, whistling, 38
swift: cave, 98; spine-tailed, 58
swordfish, 31, 32
symbiotic relationships, 107
symphylans, 39

T

tailor bird, 98
taipan, 44
tarantula, *49*
tarsier, 38
teeth, 32, *32*, 35, 49, 57
tenrec: common, 76; streaked, 76
termites, 77, 94, *94*; compass, 94; macrotermes, 94
tern, 70; arctic, 110
tiger: Bengal, 75; man-eating, 57; reproduction, 77; Siberian, *25*, 26
tinamou, 75
Tindaria callistiformis, 77
toad, 65; American, 75; *Bufo marinus*, 84; poisonous, 49, 84; reproduction, 75
tongue, *33*, 35, 37
Torpedo nobilianna, 50, 52
tortoise, Galapagos, 9, 108
trout, 60
tuna, bluefin, 60
turtle, 42; box, 60; defensive shell, *40, 42*; green, 77; loggerhead, 75; sea, 60, 77; wood, *40*
tusks, *16*, 32, *32*, 35, 38

W

walrus, 35
wasp: mason, 98; potter, 77, 98; spider-hunting, 27
water fleas, 107
weasel: least, 26; long-tailed, *82*
weaver, golden, *96*
weaverbird, *96*, *97*, 98
weaverfish, poisonous, 49
whale: baleen, 110; blue, 9, 16, *18*, 60, 62–3, 75, 77, 102, 110; bottle-nosed, 62; fin, 67; humpback, 110; killer, 55, 57, 62; migration, 110; narwhal, 32; reproduction, 75, 76, 77; sperm, 62, 108
whale shark, *18*, 21
wildebeeste, 8, 115
wolf, *54*, 57
wood louse, 39
woodpecker, pileated, 98
wood turtle, *40*
worms: earthworm, 109, *109*, 115; marine proboscis, 31
wren, short-billed marsh, *99*

Y

yak, *37*, 38

Z

zebra, 8, *86*, 87, 115
zebra fish, 49
zorilla, 52, 85

Picture Credits

Bets Anderson Bailly, p.72 (left); Chris Boylan, p.30, p.50 (top); Betty K Bruce, p.111; M. Bruce, p.20; Richard Day, p.36, p.67 (right), p.72 (right), p.73, p.81 (below); Tim Delong, p.26, p.113; John Ebeling, p.106, p.107 (right); Travis Evans, p.55; Jay Foreman, p.13, p.51 (left); Russell R Grundke, p.43 (top), p.103; Mike and Elvan Habicht, p.31; Ron P Jaffe, p.105 (below); Martha McBride, p.64 (right); D and I MacDonald, p.92, Joe McDonald, p.9, p.15, p.16, p.19 (left), p.23, p.25, p.29, p.32, p.33, p.40 (left), p.40 (right), p.42, p.44, p.49 (below), p.53, p.56 (top), p.63, p.64 (left), p.66, p.67 (left), p.69 (below), p.71, p.75, p.80 (top), p.81 (top), p.81 (centre), p.83, p.84 (below), p.85, p.86 (below), p.87, p.96 (right), p.98 (right), p.108, p.114 (below), p.119; Joe and Carol McDonald, p.59; Margo Moss, p.77; Christian Mundt, p.54; Richard T Nowitz, p.94; Photri inc, p.49 (top), p.50 (below), p.58, p.74, p.91, p.105 (top); Photri inc, Irwin, p.27, p.35, p.37 (top), p.45 (below), p.46 (top), p.46 (below); Photri inc, B Kulik, p.78; Photri inc, Leonard Lee Rue III, p.47, p.56 (below); Ann Purcell, p.12, p.17, p.22, p.57 (top), p.86 (top), p.96 (left), p.97, p.104, p.118; Carl Purcell, p.10, p.28, p.38, p.52, p.57 (below), p.60, p.68, p.116; Gary I Rothstein, p.117; Leonard Lee Rue III, p.24, p.45 (top), p.82, p.114 (top); Marcus Schneck, p.7, p.8, p.11, p.14, p.21, p.34, p.37 (right), p.39 (top), p.41, p.43 (below), p.61, p.62, p.65, p.70, p.76, p.84 (top), p.88 (left), p.88 (right), p.90, p.98 (left), p.101, p.110, p.112 (top), p.115; Lorraine O Schultz, p.112 (below), Gregory K Scott, p.39 (below), p.48, p.51 (right), p.69 (top), p.80 (below), p.89, p.93 (top), p.93 (below), p.95, p.99, p.100 (top), p.100 (below); Curt Smith, p.107 (left); C Strock, p.37 (left), p.102; Unicorn Stock Photos, Clark Coleman, p.19 (right); Unicorn Stock Photos, Dick Keen, p.18; Les Van, p.79.